Daddy Trails

Three Wishes, Three fathers, and a DNA Fairy-tale

Daddy Trails

Three wishes, three fathers, and a DNA fairy-tale.

Elizabeth Manzanares Wenig

©2022 Elizabeth Manzanares Wenig
All rights reserved.

Some names have been changed to protect the privacy of individuals. No part of this book may be reproduced in any form whatsoever, whether by graphic, visual, electronic, film, microfilm, tape recording, or any other means, without prior written permission of the publisher, except in the case of brief passages embodied in critical reviews and articles.

Website: www.lizzysfeatherpen.com

ISBN: 979-8-9873178-1-5
Isabella Castile Publishers

Cover art by Shonna Hilliard
Cover design by Gary Wenig

Printed in the United States of America

10 9 8 7 6 5 4 3 2 1

DEDICATION

I dedicate this book to Ernestina Coker, my Tia Tina. She is the first person who grabbed my attention as if calling to me across the years and miles. The first name I read, the first question I asked, and the first time I realized I wasn't whom I thought I was.

Tia Tina has inspired me with the never-ending love and acceptance she has extended to me from the very beginning of my journey. She is a bridge to my father, a link to our family, and a joy and delight in my heart. I love you forever, Tia Tina.

Table of Contents

ACKNOWLEDGMENTS ix
Prologue..1
Daddy Mac 3
Chapter 1 4
Chapter 2 10
Chapter 3 13
Chapter 4 15
Chapter 5 18
Chapter 6 27
Chapter 7 30
Chapter 8 33
Chapter 9 36
Chapter 10 40
Chapter 11 49
Chapter 12 59
Chapter 13 63
Chapter 14 65
Chapter 15 73
Chapter 16 84
Chapter 17 88
Chapter 18 91
Chapter 19 98
Chapter 20 103
Chapter 21 109
Chapter 22 114
Chapter 23 119
Frank..124
Chapter 24 125
Chapter 25 132

Chapter 26	141
Chapter 27	150
Papa Joe	155
Chapter 28	156
Chapter 29	159
Chapter 30	163
Chapter 31	168
Chapter 32	182
Chapter 33	188
Chapter 34	190
Chapter 35	193
Chapter 36	200
Epilogue	202
About The Author	203
Endnotes	204

ACKNOWLEDGMENTS

There are so many people who have helped me in the birthing of this book. Those who have labored with me cheered me on and encouraged me when I was certain no one would ever want to read my story. Those who gave me advice and suggestions. Those who dared to say, "um, are you sure you want to put that in." Those who contributed stories of the father I never knew.

Heartfelt thanks to my husband, Gary, who is not only my moral support but my go-to tech guy. To my daughter Cyndi who combined her knowledge and talents of genealogy and editing not only to help me with this book but without whom I would never have found my father. To my boys Chad and Henry whom each brought a magical element into my life and helped make me who I am today. To my granddaughter Elli who freely gave her sweet support and sounding board.

Dear friends, Janet, Linda, Dorothy, and a few others also kept me going with their input, contributions, and inquiries, "How's the book coming?" "Are you finished yet?" "I can't wait to read it." I love and appreciate your loyalty. You know who you are.

A special heartfelt thank you to all three of my families the McKees: Dorothy Kay, you were a lifeboat in my childhood; the Ewings: to my Aunt Rebecca Ewing (you will always be my auntie) for your courage and honesty, for shining a light into our dark closet. And the Manzanares: Randy, you gave me the gift of hope by taking my hand and including me even when we didn't know where we were going. And the many other Manzanares cousins and relatives who have graciously contributed not only to this book but to my life by sharing stories and photographs of my new family, and my new father. I quite literally could not have done it without you.

*To my Lord and Savior Jesus Christ Who guided
and protected me through the brambles of my
childhood and steered the course to my happy
fairy-tale ending.*

PROLOGUE

As I stand upon this side of the chasm of time and look back over my life a great swelling of gratitude rises up within me like a transparent cloud. Its misty essence touches my heart and I know that I am truly thankful not only for the light and happy times but for the dark episodes of my life. I have learned there must be opposition in all things.

We do not conquer evil by hiding it away in a secret chamber of our hearts. We overcome and vanquish wickedness by exposing it to the Light thus revealing its true nature: the cowardly craven and corrupted creature that it has always been and will forever be.

The yearning for my father planted there by my Creator has been a driving force all these years. It has taken me through shadowy paths that could have been the destruction of me had my Savior not been there, too. Only He could have saved me from the evil designs of men and brought me out on the other side distilled and refined into a better person.

The search for my father truly is a fairy-tale story. I traveled through the dismal malevolent heartache and heartbreak of brambles and briars and emerged on a resplendent mountaintop with peace and happiness upon me as a cloak and love burrowed within my soul.

Finding my father has completed me in a way nothing else could have. I have come to him not only with myself but with my children, my children's children, and their children. Three generations of my posterity have come into his family circle. The hearts of the fathers have truly been turned to their children and the hearts of the children to their fathers. (Malachi 4:6) The great circle of life has played out in mine.

As you journey through the seasons of my story with me remember that after we endure the dark, we come into the light. After my trials came my reward. My fairy-tale comes true.

DADDY MAC

CHAPTER 1

"Shame, Despair, Solitude! These had been her teachers - stern and wild ones - and they had made her strong but taught her much amiss."
Nathanial Hawthorne   "The Scarlet Letter"

My grandfather Robert died of a broken heart in the icy cold month of December six weeks before I was born. I mourn for him still, the grandfather I never knew. And I mourn for my mother, for now, she was truly alone. At 21 years of age, Emma Eleanor Bryant was no stranger to hard times. She rarely spoke of it, but my imagination hears the desolate Colorado wind howling in sympathy and sees the snow piled high against the sides of the little house as if the drifts were giving it a hug to console the lone occupant. Mama.

The entire Bryant family blamed Mama for Grandpa Robert's death; a burden she carried throughout her life. Grandma Minnie had died six years prior catapulting Mama into adulthood. Her role of chief cook and bottle washer ill-fitted her scant fifteen years of age. Her younger siblings, one older brother, and her father looked to Mama for hot and hearty meals, clean and mended clothing, and moral motherly support.

Mama quit school. She was a woman now with a woman's responsibilities. She needed adult props and grown-up habits. She started to smoke and that was the beginning of the end.

When it became evident that I was a reality and not a maybe, Mama lived the proverbial scarlet letter. She wore shame as a sign that she was a fallen woman and became a social and family outcast. Grandpa Robert did not bear his family's disgrace and humiliation well. His health deteriorated resulting in a death that not only added further guilt to Mama's burden but placed her in a precarious position. Now, she was truly alone.

Mama lived in Pueblo but when her confinement was upon her, she traveled to Denver. I was delivered at Booth Memorial Hospital, one more fatherless child in the world. Mama filled out the forms and my name became Ida Elizabeth Ewing. Immediately after my birth, she went back to Pueblo. It always puzzled me as to why she would leave her home and travel to a strange city, a strange hospital, and strange caretakers to give birth. I would not learn the speculative answer to that question for seventy-four years.

Mama got an infection a few weeks after my birth and required surgery. During her recuperation, other family members helped with my care, but that didn't mean they had changed their minds about me or my untimely arrival upon the earth. The world would be a better place without this illegitimate girl-child and Mama--unmarried and without any kind of financial or familial support--would certainly be better off.

Mama's aunt, bold and with righteous conviction, took me into an unoccupied unheated bedroom, laid me on the bed, unwrapped my blanket, bared my chest, and opened the window to the bitter relentless icy Colorado March winds. Aunty couldn't comprehend why Mama insisted on keeping this child who had disrupted the Bryant family and killed her brother, Grandpa Robert. She was certain Mama's situation would be much improved if I were gone.

She nearly succeeded. Pneumonia gripped and ripped through my tiny body, but God had other plans for me. I survived but a variety of respiratory illnesses revisited me countless times during my life.

*"Childhood should be carefree, playing in the sun;
not living a nightmare in the darkness of the soul."*
Dave Pelzer, <u>A Child Called "It"</u>

A good babysitter has been hard to find throughout the ages. Mama needed childcare while she worked as a waitress and had considered herself fortunate to find a woman with children. I was around two years old, and Mama thought the other children would be good for me. I don't know how long the arrangement had been going on before tragedy struck.

I remember Mama holding me in hysterics while an ambulance siren loudly blared to a stop outside. The caretaker had fed me hot peppers; the inside of my mouth and throat were blistered and raw. The episode left my tongue split, sensitive, and an impaired sense of taste for the rest of my life. The woman was later arrested for the attempted murder of one of her own children.

Mama and I rented a tiny upstairs apartment while she waitressed across the street. The bedroom was a small enclosure where the walls touched the bed on three sides. At the foot of the bed, a curtain hung for privacy from the small sitting room. Since babysitters obviously could not be trusted, I stayed alone. After all, Mama was just across the street. She came over on breaks to check on me.

One night I heard the old door knob slowly turn. Someone stepped inside the room and walked slowly across the creaking floor. I sat up in bed, the tiny cubicle black as pit.

"Mama?"," I said softly. "Mama?"

I stared blindly at the curtain, waiting. A hand reached into the small enclosure and lifted the fabric. A man stood peering into the tiny bedroom area, and strangely enough I wasn't afraid. He turned on the light and smiled. He was all good feelings, and gentle eyes. He cautiously extended his hand and within his grip, a little toy dog peeked at me. I reached out, took the dog, and drew it under my chin in a child's hug. He turned out to be Mama's little brother home from the Navy and I loved him instantly. I only saw him a few times in my life but I never forgot how wonderful and safe he made me feel.

> *"Elephants love reunions. They recognize one another after years and years of separation and greet each other with wild, boisterous joy. There's bellowing and trumpeting, ear flapping and rubbing. Trunks entwine."*
> Jennifer Richard Jacobson, Small as an Elephant

I was raised by Mama and my stepfather, Lloyd (Mac) McKee. Or, Daddy Mac, as I now call him to differentiate him from my other two dads.

Shortly after the hot pepper incident when I was about two years old Daddy Mac was traveling cross country and swaggered into the restaurant where Mama waitressed. He was a rolling stone always taking jobs that afforded travel. His charismatic nature, fun personality, non-judgmental attitude, and willingness to take on a mother and her child were irresistible, so mama quit her job and went off into the sunset with her Prince Charming tagging me along.

We landed in Nebraska where Daddy Mac and Mama operated a small bar and grill, and he was a master at running it. The window boasted "Mac's" painted across the glass. He had a never-ending supply of stories, jokes and advice and even entertained the patrons with guitar and song.

Mama ran the short-order grill. Her cooking skills were minimal despite the fact she had overseen a family household since age fifteen. I loved rearranging the spice cans behind the little cooking counter. It was my own sequestered world and became my personal private space.

Our living quarters were in the small damp basement with a mattress on the cement floor. When I caught croup, I was confined to the family bed for days and cried to be up arranging my spices. The horrid gray medicine was abominable. I can still smell the heaved contents of someone's stomach coming from that bottle.

What child can resist a circus?! Not me. The bar and grill was open, so Mama and Daddy Mac were busy. Too busy to take me to the traveling circus that had taken the small Nebraska town by storm the night before. My established domain was anywhere in Daddy Mac's bar, Mama's kitchen, in the basement slash living-sleeping quarters, or right out front on the sidewalk where I drew chalk doodles for hours on end.

The circus was making camp right down the street in a big vacant lot. I was an iron shard drawn to the lodestone incapable of resisting. Mama's admonition to stay in front of the bar went right out of my head and into the ether. I could hear them down there, men shouting, trucks sputtering, horns honking, women shuffling, children laughing, and…what was that? Could it be? A gusty roar trumpeted through the air. My mouth flew open, I dropped the chalk and walked over my sidewalk masterpiece slowly at first, then faster until I was flying down the street.

An elephant! I could hear an elephant! I approached the busy lot with eyes scanning back and forth trying to get a bearing on the distinctive sound broadcasting through the pandemonium of setting up a circus. People were everywhere, each one focusing on their own task. I turned a corner and came face to face with a horse. Panic welled up inside me; I froze. I hadn't known I was terrified of horses, having never met one before. The pony stood quietly watching me as its owner gently stroked his mane and rubbed his face. I quietly backed up until the horse and his owner walked in the other direction.

At that same moment, a great uproar erupted further into the circus lot. People were running toward me and around me like the rushing water of a river around boulders. Behind the crowd came the owner of that marvelous piercing trumpet I had heard earlier.

The elephant! He sauntered casually without a leash or tether as if he were out on a Sunday stroll. My heart soared. He was magnificent. I walked toward him; he walked toward me. His curious nose reached out to me; my hand extended to him. For one second, we touched. I could scarcely breathe. For just a moment I was lost in his gentle eyes.

Suddenly, someone grabbed me from behind and pulled me into their arms. The elephant shied, reared up, and let loose a colossal roar. The person carrying me began to run; I watched men surround the elephant casting ropes and ensnaring the enraged animal with beautiful eyes.

That night Daddy Mac's bar was packed. Townspeople and circus citizens alike gathered to hear him tell and retell my so-called brush with death by taming the wild, rogue elephant. It became one of Daddy Mac's staples in his story repertoire.

CHAPTER 2

*"To her, the name of father
was another name for love."*
Fanny Fern

Daddy Mac, a rogue freewheeling bachelor, was learning to be a dad. He was trying to fit into a pair of brand-new tight ill-fitting shoes. It would take a while to break them in.

Eventually, we landed in Kansas City. We lived in two separate cramped apartments, neither of which had a bedroom. In the first two-room apartment the main room contained a chair, a dresser, a bed, and a sofa where I slept. There was a tiny adjacent kitchen. The bathroom which we shared with the landlady and one other tenant was out in the common hall and up the stairs. This proved problematic when a kindergartner's small bladder is combined with a lack of control over bodily functions and an excruciatingly long stairway.

Daddy Mac loved the outdoors and animals and fostered that love in me. One day he brought home an injured pigeon from work which we nursed back to health. Much to my delight, she roosted on the bedsprings during her recuperation.

Daddy Mac spent a summer in Minnesota as a fishing guide. That was my first experience outside our smokey, stuffy rooms, and it sought out and sparked a love for all things alfresco; the cold pristine lakes splashing with fish and turtles, the tall trees swaying and singing in the breeze and the smell of fresh pine, the chipmunks teasing me by coming close then scampering away before I could catch them. Mother Nature took up residence in my heart and never left.

I had fallen in love with my Daddy Mac. His easy-going ways, quick infectious laugh, charismatic personality, and generosity of spirit drew me in. He held me on his lap, tickled me, "whiskered" me, let me play with the fishing lures while we were in the boat, taught me to disengage a fish from the hook, and prepared me to stand on my own two feet. Literally and figuratively. I felt like his little girl. And, best of all, he made Mama happy.

Daddy Mac worked at Darby's in the heart of the Kansas City stockyards and Mama worked at Intercollegiate Press in Kansas City. Mama dropped me off at the downtown Salvation Army Daycare and picked me up after work on her way home. Her job was within walking distance from our apartment, but a long way for my short young legs. Winter wind tunneled through the canyons of high-rise buildings often making our walk bitter cold.

I didn't especially like it at the daycare. It felt cold and impersonal and the woman in charge of my group showed blatant partiality to her own daughter. One day she imperiously humiliated one of my friends in front of the other children. I don't know if that experience took root in my own psyche and helped me develop a super sense of empathy or if I had innate compassion. Perhaps a little of both.

In 1951 Kansas City experienced a nightmare flood from which it never fully recovered. Daddy Mac and the men of Darby's answered the civic call to fill sandbags to try to control the Mighty Missouri and Kansas Rivers that converged to make a giant swell of water. The men sweltered in the hot days and nights of July, but the surge would not be stopped. The historical stockyards of Kansas City were covered with filthy, swirling floodwater bearing the bodies of 5,000 cattle. The suffocating stench blanketed the city, encroaching upon the citizens' fear of disease. Our own apartment reeked from the deadly reminder.

Daddy Mac stood ankle-deep in the muck with his coworkers looking at the swirling mass floating downstream. Pieces of the debris consisted of every conceivable item, automobiles half-submerged with windows gone, buildings broken, furniture shattered, trees fragmented, and animals dead.

Daddy Mac looked, then looked again. There on top of a furniture flotilla eddying down the floodwater sat a small dog. Terrified, filthy, cold, and wet, the dog looked at the men, yipped, and wagged his tail. Seeing life in the midst of death, Daddy Mac and the men called to the dog. Without hesitation as if waiting for an opportunity, he jumped valiantly into the murky depths. Daddy Mac cheered as the dog emerged from his dive and began swimming toward the sandbag shore. The swift current carried the dog downstream as he paddled toward safety. The men tried to run with the water encouraging the tiring dog, trying to bolster his efforts with theirs. With each sucking step of their boots in the mud, they could see the dog bobbing more and more beneath the surface. Then, his feet stopped paddling like he had used his last morsel of energy. He sunk into the foul and filthy floodwater.

Daddy Mac cried as he related the story. I cried, too.

CHAPTER 3

"They come to you in sheep's clothing, but inwardly they are ravenous wolves."   Matthew 7:15

John was tall and lanky. A tower of filth. We sometimes went to some friend's house for Daddy Mac and Mama to play cards. This couple had several boys and no girls. The natural rowdy bravado of boys always made me withdraw into shyness. They were all older than me watching television in the living room; I meandered back and forth bored and restless from the living room to the kitchen through a dark spare room. The parents were seated at the kitchen table engrossed in the card game, but John was the fifth wheel. He prowled the house. Silently. Relentlessly. A predator disguised as a pal.

On one of my trips through the spare room, he snatched me up into his arms. He held me tight; his foul breath assaulted my cheek. He cradled me in the crook of his arm, his other hand lay caressingly on my calf then crept slowly up the inside of my leg under my dress, his fingers worming into my panties.

I was mortified, terrified. Alarm bells rang throughout my heart and mind. I was repulsed beyond imagining. When his fingers began to hurt me, I pushed away from him using his chest for leverage. I caught him by surprise, and he dropped me. Instantly he grabbed my hand and put it to the front of his pants. I jerked away and ran into the living room. The boys engrossed in their television program didn't even look up. John walked into the room, and I ran around him toward the kitchen. I planted myself beside Mama at the table. My heart was racing. I was too terrified and confused for tears.... they would come later. I didn't get two inches from Mama the rest of the evening.

The next day we were stopped at a gas station; Daddy Mac was outside the car supervising the refueling, Mama sat in the front, and I was in the backseat. I have no idea what prompted it. Perhaps the horror just could not remain within me any longer. I burst into tears and sobbingly retold the events of the previous evening. Mama was stunned; an outraged mama-bear look came into her eyes. She rolled down the window and said "Lloyd, get in here." Mama always called Daddy Mac Lloyd. She never ever told him what to do, so the shock of that alone got his attention, and combined with the commanding tone of her voice he immediately paid the attendant and got into the car.

Mama recounted what I had told her using somewhat more adult language. Daddy Mac went into a rage. Not once did either of them ever question the truth of my story. Weeks before John had given Daddy Mac a charming tiny gold locket to give to me. I loved it. The necklace disappeared and John's name was never mentioned in our house again.

This episode with John could have been so much worse, and as I will discover during the course of my life, angels accompany me. I truly believe David's Psalm 91:11:

> *"For he shall give his angels charge over thee, to keep thee in all thy ways."*

CHAPTER 4

"...he that is drunk is not a man:
because he is so long void of Reason, that
distinguishes a Man from a Beast."   *William Penn*

  I grew and changed and matured day by day until one day I recognized it. Not all at once. Inch by agonizing inch I realized there was something amiss with Daddy Mac and Mama.

    When the first shadow of darkness slid over my inner sunshine, I wasn't quite sure what had happened. A pall of uncertainty was in the air. Daddy Mac's happy-go-lucky ways would disintegrate into domineering, controlling, mean unrecognizable acts of shouting, obscenities, and violence. Mama's mothering instincts gave way to whirlwinds of excited behavior, laughter that wasn't laughter at all, but a hollow sound reverberating around her insecurities. I'm sure that darkness had always been there lurking in the background waiting for me to catch up; finally, I did.

    It took many more years before I would realize that liquor was the catalyst for their transformation. Alcohol was behind the abrupt and sudden change in them. One moment Mama was, well, my mama. Loving. Smiling. Cuddling. The next moment she was a stranger. Her eyes lost their beautiful sparkle dimmed and shrouded with something dark and ominous. A stranger looked at me through Mama's eyes.

Forever after I could tell when anyone was drinking by looking into their eyes.

Drinking for Daddy Mac and Mama was their entertainment, their hobby, their life. Smoking was an acrimonious malignant presence. Whether we were frequenting the local bars or in our tiny apartment, I began to take every opportunity to escape its choking fog by going outside. I know now that smoke was the catalyst behind my many trips to the Children's Mercy croup tents.

Daddy Mac and Mama loved to party. Although most of the time they drank at the local bar, or at home, occasionally they would go "out on the town" as they put it. New Year's Eve was one of those occasions. It had been planned for days. Uncle Bill (Daddy Mac's brother) and his wife, Aunt Mary, were coming and were to meet up at the restaurant. The landlady slash babysitter slived in an upstairs apartment, close to that bathroom I mentioned. The plan was for her to come down regularly to check on me. Although, I'm quite sure that "regularly" morphed into rarely. My perk was getting to go to sleep in Mama and Daddy Mac's bed instead of the couch.

The big New Year's Eve event came and with it came an earache. I had them frequently, and, of course, it had to be this night. The pain pierced my ear and head and neck; I cried, and Mama said it would be ok. I'd go to sleep, and everything would be better. Daddy Mac blew smoke into my ear, Mama stuffed in some cotton, and they left. This was the first time I had the smoke-in-the-ear remedy, but it wouldn't be the last. I blocked out the rest of that night, but it would be filled in years later at Daddy Mac's funeral.

Uncle Bill was the father of two of my cherished girl cousins along with two boys. Their household was completely opposite of mine. With a family of six came fun, giggling, pranks, the comradery only siblings can generate and the atmosphere of mischief only boys can conjure. I occasionally got to stay with them a few days and it was always a highlight in my year.

Uncle Bill was Daddy Mac's younger and only living brother. He took me aside at Daddy Mac's funeral and began with an apology which took me by surprise. He recounted a story of when he and Aunt Mary were meeting my folks to usher in the New Year. They came by our apartment, but Daddy Mac and Mama had already left. The apartment door was unlocked; Uncle Bill knew I was supposed to be there, but I was not in the bed. After some searching, they found me hiding in the closet crying. He and Aunt Mary were shocked not only that I was alone, but that I was sick and alone and afraid.

They put me to bed, tried to comfort me, and left. He said he never got over that night. That he should have talked to his big brother about it but didn't. He said that he and Aunt Mary had thought about and discussed taking me away from Daddy Mac to live with him and his family, but I was legally out of reach. After all, he couldn't take something away from Daddy Mac that wasn't his. Nevertheless, he told me with tears in his eyes that he regretted not doing something to help me.

This was one of several enlightening moments in my adult life when I realized there had been other people aware of my situation.

CHAPTER 5

"Life's great happiness is to be convinced we are loved". Victor Hugo "Les Miserables"

An antidote to the nightmare in which I lived was my grandparents. Henry and Lizzy McKee. Daddy Mac announced we would be going to see them that weekend and it was a long, long week for me as I waited to meet my new Grandpa and Grandma. I was so excited Saturday morning I jumped off my couch-bed and sprinted out the apartment door and up the stairs to the community bathroom. By the time we were on our way, I was spit and polished to the best of my kindergarten self.

We were going to the "Land of Oz" which made it ever more exciting. The old two-lane Kansas highway had a stretch that went up and down in roller coaster fashion making me sick with nausea and occasionally, vomiting, a malady that plagued Daddy Mac my entire childhood.

It didn't dampen my spirits. Just think of it...GRANDPARENTS!! Actual flesh and blood Grandma. A real Grandpa. I couldn't fathom it.

I was so caught up in my own delight, I didn't think of how Mama must have felt until years later. Both her parents had been dead for many years. Daddy Mac's mom and dad would now be Mama's, too.

It seemed like forever driving from our city apartment to Grandma's country farm. After hours on the road Daddy Mac said that if we had been in New York, we would still be in the city. I never forgot that impromptu geography lesson and decided right then that I never wanted to live in New York.

We pulled off the dirt road and parked alongside a fence. Behind the fence stood a remarkable house. It had a screened-in porch—a new and unimaginable feat of architecture to my cramped apartment template. Just outside the front door stood an older couple. The woman wore a housedress covered with a floral printed apron. And, perched on her head was a perky little cap. She was smiling and her eyes shone with a sweetness I didn't recognize. She entered my soul with a power I had never experienced. Like a warm blanket in a blizzard. Was this a fairy Godmother? From that moment on my heart was hers forever.

Beside her, a man stood quietly dressed in striped overalls. I had never seen such a thing. So, this was a grandpa. And he was mine.

They started walking toward the car through the large expanse of yard. Daddy Mac opened the gate. Suddenly overcome with shyness I slipped behind Mama afraid to face these new people in my life but still grinning like a monkey. After they greeted Daddy Mac and met Mama, Grandma Lizzy bent over, put her arm around me, and said, "This must be Beth."

I was enveloped in the first of a lifetime of grandma hugs and I felt like flying. And as if that didn't send my soul soaring, I learned that my new grandma's name was Elizabeth, too. That sealed it. I was bonded to her for life. I named my daughter after her, a legacy of love.

Grandpa's name, Henry, ended up being a family name, too. I named one of my sons Henry and he, in turn, named his son Henry. A heritage of Henrys.

My grandparents were a safe harbor for me. I loved spending time during the occasional summer at their farm. I couldn't wait to get out of our smokey, stuffy crowded apartment and partake of the big farmhouse, sprawling hills and pastures and creek and barns, and even the outhouse. The chickens, cows, pigs, dogs, cats, gardens, and tractors were an endless source of joy and freedom. Besides the exquisite happiness of being with my very own Grandpa and Grandma, there were cousins thrown into the mix. Think of it…cousins!

The cousins also came to Grandma Lizzy's in the summer. I especially loved my girl cousins. I'm pretty sure the three of them spent a lot more time there than I did. Shirley was the oldest and a fashion role model. She and her brother belonged to Daddy Mac's only sister, Aunt Lucille and her husband Uncle Jim. Dorothy Kay, who was my age and became mi Hermana, mi amiga, and my sister-cousin, and her little sister, were Uncle Bill's girls. Oh, the adventures we had.

Our bed was in the attic which we explored, screaming with giggly delight over the ghosts in the next room whom we imagined played the old discarded dusty organ whenever the notion took them. We piled into the featherbed at night. Under the sheets lie a sea of feathers embraced in their ticking, a downy comfort of love that fills in all the spaces and holds us safe and warm in the dark of the night. My imagination heard the melodious cry of geese flying low over Grandpa's harvested fields, coming to surrender to the ancient inevitable ritual of giving themselves for the food and warmth of others. I felt the magic of life flowing from one being into another.

Grandma Lizzy crafted this featherbed. She plucked all the down, lovingly stuffed the ticked cavity, hour after hour, plucking and stuffing, plucking and stuffing. We don't lie on the bed, the bed holds and enfolds us, the bed mothers us, the feathers rise up around us. I didn't know about my cousins, but I felt protected in a nest of peace. My body sinks heavily into blissful slumber while my mind soars through the night sky with the clouds, a faint honking somewhere in the distance.

The cousins and I took turns using the chamber pot and shared the repugnant duty of emptying it in the outhouse the next morning. It would be many years before inside plumbing was installed.

We "helped" Grandma Lizzy cook on the woodstove and wash dishes by pumping water with a beautiful tiny red pump that Grandpa had mounted on the countertop by the dry sink. It was very modern to have the "piped in" water, but we still had to empty the dishpan out the back door onto the weeping willow. I love willows to this day and admire my own Alice as she sways to the rhythm of the valley out my back door.

Grandma Lizzy continued to wear an apron and a cap every day. I was thrilled at wearing them, too, every time I swept the kitchen. She kept them on a nail behind the kitchen door; I always put them back after my chores and told them goodbye each time I had to leave and go back to the city.

From day one, my grandparents accepted me as their own. They were my family, and I was theirs. During these delightful summer days and sometimes on holidays, the McKee link was forged in my heart beginning with Grandpa Henry and Grandma Lizzy, through my aunts and uncles, cousins, to Daddy Mac, and finally down to me. I felt anchored.

Grandma Lizzy's house became the shore of my drowning childhood. When I was there, I was free of smoke-filled rooms, vulgar stories, and mysterious late-night under-the-cover groanings. Dorothy Kay lived just a mile or so away from Grandma, so Aunt Mary brought all her kids over when I was there. I bonded immediately with Dorothy Kay. Grandma afforded us a great deal of self-governance which we mostly honored.

One of our favorite pastimes besides playing "Bride" was cooking. Dorothy Kay and I constructed elaborate kitchens from items discovered laying around the farm. We used boards and wooden boxes for cabinets, empty coffee cans for dishes, and sturdy sticks for spoons.

Dorothy Kay and I were banned from Grandma's kitchen hand pump, but the main pump was in the ground just outside the kitchen door. It usually took both of us to coax water up the pipes and out the spigot. I loved that pump even after the winter she (I always thought of the pump as female) turned against me and immobilized my tongue against her frozen metal pipe.

One sunny afternoon Grandma left Dorothy Kay and me to our own imaginings, and we were seriously involved in making, baking, and eating (pretend, of course) the proverbial mud pie. Grandma's pies were unarguably the best in the county; her apple pie was legendary. It wasn't really a pie. It was a vision of warm cinnamony, spicey, sweet, gooey apples from the tree out by the sweet corn patch wrapped in a blanket of flakey lard crust sprinkled with sugar. Pure heaven. Grandma said it was a cross between a pie and a cobbler. In my mind, it became Apple Cob

Pie and I asked for and got it every time I was there and daydreamed about it when I wasn't.

How could Dorothy Kay and I transform our ordinary mud pies into a similitude of Apple Cob Pie? As a fat hen searched for a way out of the chicken yard into Grandma's paradisiacal garden of ripening tomatoes, the answer struck us. We looked at one another and exclaimed in unison, "EGGS!".

The idea of asking permission lay hidden somewhere in Beeton's "Manners for Polite Society" but was not privy to an actual existence in children's minds. At least not ours. We needed something in which to gather the eggs, and we both agreed one of Grandma's housekeeping caps would be perfect. We crept silently into the kitchen, grabbed a cap off the nail behind the door, and ran off toward the chicken house certain that this was the fait accompli that would catapult our pies into stardom. Surely the egg was the culinary secret waiting to transform mere mud into an extraordinary Apple Cob Pie.

The chicken house was new territory. Lewis and Clark territory. Seeing the hens hunting and pecking in their chicken yard on the other side of the fence was not anything at all like being in their house plotting to steal their future progeny. Not being able to decide who would enter first, we went through the door together holding hands.

A row of nests extended across the back of the hen house with roosts between them and the door. The air was filled with chicken dust dancing in the sunbeams streaking across the room. Our plan was to rush in, grab a couple of eggs and dash out before the hens knew what was happening. We expected the nests to be empty of chickens and full of eggs. That turned out to be only half true.

Most of the nests were occupied. The hens sat proprietarily on their little chicken thrones daring anyone to even think about snatching an egg. We crept around the roosts clinging to one another's hands, our eyes locked with chicken eyes. The hens began to cackle. It wasn't the sweet little song we had heard them sing while scrapping for bugs and scratching in the dirt. This was an alarm, plain and simple and the hens were sounding it with all the chicken passion they could muster.

There was one nest directly in front of us void of chickens and it was full of eggs. We simultaneously let go of each other and reached into the nest with lightning speed, snatched the eggs, and having forgotten Grandma's cap in our own little kitchen, we stuffed the eggs into our shorts pockets and sunsuit tops then turned and ran.

We reached our makeshift kitchen heady and giggling with success. Our intent was to appropriate one egg for the pie because after considerable discussion, disagreement, and finally consensus that is what the Apple Cob Mud Pie recipe called for. We unloaded our precious contraband from pockets and sunsuit tops slowly with great care and were delighted not one was broken. Not even a crack. Our astonishment exploded as we counted the eggs. FIVE! Five eggs, far more than our meager imaginations, cunning plotting, and daring execution ever dreamed of.

Eager to get the Apple Cob Mud Pie into the oven, a sheltered hole under a pile of rocks, we took our coffee can to the well, coordinated our efforts, pumped a can of water, then added the right amount of dirt. Dorothy Kay and I took turns stirring with our sticks imitating Grandma beating up breakfast pancakes. Then, the crowning moment; together we cracked the egg and plopped it into the black batter. It sat on top for a moment, then disappeared into the gooey mixture.

Spurred on by the promise of culinary success, we alternately blended, beat, whipped, and whisked the beautiful black Cob Pie into the perfect consistency. We looked at it with Grandma-like scrutiny and declared it ready for the oven. The only thing missing was apples. But Grandpa strictly forbade any climbing of the apple tree. Although we would disregard that mandate later in childhood for the time being the Apple Cob Mud Pie would be devoid of its namesake as there were no apples to be found under the tree.

During the "baking" time, we tidied up the kitchen and then sat down on some firewood to discuss the future of our remaining eggs. We voiced and discarded several ideas and then hit upon the winner. I'm not sure who thought of it first, but we both enthusiastically agreed upon the solution. We had four eggs left. We each had two sides to our sunsuit tops. We cautiously placed the eggs in the strategic areas, examined one another, and declared ourselves beautiful and very grown-up.

The Apple Cob Mud Pie was ready to come out of the oven. We noticed that across the yard Grandma and Aunt Mary were filling up the galvanized tub with buckets of water from the well. Normally it was pressed into service for laundry but today would serve as a wading pool.

We hurriedly removed the cob pie from the oven, stashed it in the makeshift pie safe, and walked demurely toward the pool with adult aplomb, our eggs still nestled securely in our sunsuit tops. As we approached, we noticed Grandma and Aunt Mary staring at us and then slowly looking at one another. They had probably noticed how mature we looked.

Every year the grandchildren had a special project. Grandpa said this was a farm and, on a farm, everyone did their share of work. We and we alone had been assigned this task and if we did not do it, it would not get done. And that just couldn't happen. So it was, every summer we were given a mission of such magnitude that it took all the cousins working together in harmony without bickering over procedure to accomplish it. We were to paint the pool.

This was no ordinary pool. This pool was unique in all the world. This was a magical pool. Its diminutive size did not in any sense reduce its importance to the landscape of Grandpa Henry and Grandma Lizzy's front yard. Nor did it lessen the enjoyment the grandchildren experienced when walking, running or even crawling across the tiny bridge or accidentally on purpose falling into the water.

Grandpa dug out an hourglass-shaped hole no more than three or four feet at its widest and six or seven feet long then poured cement over the dirt making a watertight pool. Then Grandpa took an old running board, from a tractor or truck I never knew which, welded a curved baluster on each side. He placed it at the waist of the hourglass producing a charming little bridge across the pool. It was enchanting.

The grandchildren always looked forward to our painting project and carried it out with unbridled enthusiasm. The painting crew did not always consist of a full cohort of cousins, but each summer we carried out Grandpa's mandate with childhood determination. The last summer we were there together we painted the tiny pool; we went all out and created a rainbow masterpiece. The next winter worked its worst by freezing a crack across the cement almost as if it knew the cousins had finally outgrown the tiny pool.

As the only semblance of running water in Grandma Lizzy's house was her little red pump in the kitchen, when it came to bath time Grandpa initiated old fashion ingenuity. Bathing usually resulted in standing over a small basin using a washcloth quickly if not thoroughly just so we could say we'd bathed.

Grandpa took the evening bath to a whole new level. Grandma's living room had a "back door" that opened into a porch that was actually an add-on. It joined the house to the root cellar, had a cement floor, and slanted toward a screen door that went outside. Grandpa commandeered a small, galvanized wash tub, (much smaller than the one we used for a "swimming" pool) punched holes in the bottom and rigged it to hang from the ceiling. He hung it just a few feet inside the back screen door so the water would run right under the door to the outside flower bed. Grandpa was a genius.

We could hardly wait until evening so we could "shower". We stood under Grandpa's inventive apparatus as Grandma stepped up on her stool and dumped fresh well water into the tub. It rained down in freezing streams of elation. We loved it. Our shrieks of shivering excitement escalated as the cold water splashed down soaking not only us but Grandma as well. She good-naturedly stood at the ready with towels and hugs.

The cellar door was just a few steps away from the shower rig. Grandma stored food of all kinds in the cool, dark recess of the cellar, canned goods—jelly being my favorite—sitting on shelves, fresh apples, pears, and peaches picked carefully from the trees, and potatoes, beets, and onions dug fresh from the garden, various varieties of squash gathered from the vines all stored in bushel baskets lining the perimeter of the cellar floor.

Occasionally Grandma requested we retrieve a needed food item from the cellar. We were loath to admit we were afraid to go into the dragon's cave. The dragon being a resident black snake whom I supposed gained entry through the vent in the roof. All the girl cousins were afraid of him, but Grandma said he was our friend because he ate the mice who ate the food. The boy cousins thought it was funny and pretended to be brave, but I don't recall any of them retrieving food from the dark cavern of terror.

In all the years of valiantly going into the dragon's lair, I only saw him eye to eye a couple of times. I suppose that gives credence to the "he's more afraid of you than you are of him" adage that Grandma Lizzy always recited when it was time for one of us to fetch something from the cellar.

The old stone cellar was crafted ages ago into the hillside behind the house by family whose names I would learn years later when typing them into a genealogy program. The roof curved charmingly overhead rounded with rock originally from said hillside. I imagined the long-ago family dredging out the rock, then meticulously building the arch that would form the cellar roof. When I thought of them, they were my family. The McKee's. I claimed them. Grandma always told me I was hers. That I was one of them. That I was family. When I was with her, I believed it. I loved it. I felt like a true died-in-the-wool genuine blood granddaughter.

CHAPTER 6

"Seeing is believing, but sometimes the most real things in the world are the things we can't see."

The Conductor from <u>The Polar Express</u>

Christmas!!! I've always loved Christmas, but then, what child doesn't? I don't remember anyone telling me stories of our Savior's birth. I learned it somewhere along the way and knew it by the time we moved to the country. But while we still lived in the city Santa was my Christmas world. He was a mysterious man who was constantly happy. The man who always listened...really listened ... to children. The man who could grant wishes, make me smile, who loved animals, especially reindeer. And he could fly!!!

I loved going to Macy's at Christmas to see Santa. It was a rare treat to get to go into a store. Daddy Mac's brother, Uncle Bill and Aunt Mary, on occasion came to the city to visit. I don't remember them bringing my cousins, but it was still an indulgence to see them.

One festive evening Mama, Aunt Mary, and I were in Macy's riding up that magical escalator. The draping of Christmas was twinkling, glittering, and sparkling everywhere you looked. Suddenly, the escalator jerked to a sudden stop, and we all went tumbling backward. Mama fell hard and when she didn't get up with the rest of us, I knew something was wrong.

Mama had many days of pain and inactivity that stretched far past Christmas. Daddy Mac was furious and swore Macy's would pay. Which they eventually did.

Daddy Mac had a way of stretching the ordinary until it became extraordinary. He was a master storyteller having honed his craft in the late-night tavern atmosphere of captive listeners. One such tale grew out of a golden ring he always wore. The ring had a translucent red setting that in the course of the story had a moon rising within it. So, naturally, one of us named it his "moon ring".

We usually had Christmas at Grandma Lizzy's. I always looked forward to that with a childlike frenzy, but this year we traveled to Daddy Mac's sister, Aunt Lucille's, house for Christmas. Uncle Bill and Aunt Lucille were Daddy Mac's only living siblings and by this time they both lived in the same city about an hour from Grandpa's and Grandma Lizzy's house.

We traveled there on Christmas Eve. Daddy Mac had let me hold his ring during the trip because even if I dropped it, it wasn't going anywhere but the car's floor. It was dark and as I lay in the back seat, trying not to get car sick, I looked up at the moon. It was only half there. I held up the ring so I could look at the moon through the red setting. There really was a moon in there!

Aunt Lucille and Uncle Jim had two children, a boy and a girl. More cherished cousins. I loved playing with them, especially their girl, Shirley. She was older than Dorothy Kay and I; Dorothy Kay being Uncle Bill's oldest. It didn't matter whether we were at one of their houses or at Grandma Lizzy's we had a grand time together usually playing wedding. Except, Dorothy Kay and I could never quite figure out why Shirley always got to be the bride. Guess being older had its perks.

This Christmas bulged with food, decorations, laughter, stories, and a beautiful tree. But we kids, just tolerated everything until we got to the good part...Santa. He would arrive during that nebulous undefinable time of "after dinner".

Finally, at the end of an exasperatingly long time of expectation, the announcement was made. Santa was coming. I stood with the throng of cousins watching the door. I closed my eyes one last time and thought about my Christmas wish. I could see a beautiful "baby" buggy just the right size for my own baby—a little doll I'd had forever and cherished beyond anything. Mama and Daddy Mac had repeatedly told me I was not getting the buggy because we just didn't have room in our small apartment.

At last, Santa came through the door with his famous pack full of presents. He ho-ho-hoed and began passing out the toys. I knew there was no baby buggy in that pack. I took the small gift he handed me successfully hiding my disappointment, holding back my tears, and forcing a smile. I didn't really need that buggy anyway.

I sat on the floor amidst wrapping paper. Santa left and my cousins were all involved in their own gifts; the adults watched them like they were the best movie ever. I was fiddling with my gift--don't even remember what it was--when I realized the room was getting quiet. I looked up. Santa was coming back into the room pushing a tiny beautiful, shiny, blue baby buggy. It seemed as if the people and presents parted to make way for him. Remembering this incident later I thought it seemed like the Red Sea parting, just for Santa and that buggy.

Santa came to a stop directly in front of me and said, "Merry Christmas". I stood up scarcely breathing. I reached for the buggy handle. Just as Santa was removing his hand, I saw it. There on Santa's finger was the Moon Ring.

During these few seconds of confusion, a great surge of knowing came over me. I would not have been able to put it into words. I felt numb, my hand froze on the buggy handle. Santa laughed his final ho-ho-ho and exited the room. I stood watching him as I tried to put the puzzle together in my mind when the pieces just wouldn't fit.

On the long car ride home, the staggering emotion of the day subsided somewhat, but my mind was still muddled. The realization that Daddy Mac and Santa both wore the Moon Ring presented a whole other world of uncertainty. I finally decided I would think about it later. I cuddled my doll and thought about her buggy in the trunk. We were going to have such great walks.

CHAPTER 7

"Hope...which is whispered from Pandora's box only after all the other plagues and sorrows had escaped, is the best and last of all things."
Ian Caldwell

When I hit the third grade we moved to a slightly better apartment a few blocks across town. We had our very own bathroom which evoked squeals of delight not only from me but from Mama as well. And the bed! The bed was a magical mystery. It folded up into the wall! If you didn't know it was there, well, you'd never know!! When it was pulled down out of its secret chamber, the bed was just a few inches from the couch, my bed. This would prove somewhat educational.

Our tenement building sat on a hill; our apartment being in the rear. The front door of the building was on ground level but by the time we entered our unit we were two stories from the ground. An alley separated our building from another one just like it. As is the way with apartment buildings in the city, there was an abundance of children.

I was innately shy at school and needed coaxing to participate. I purposely gave wrong answers in class so as to blend in with the group and not call attention to myself. I was frequently bullied on my short walk home after school. One day a small group of three girls drove me into our small two-room apartment with mean and ugly words; their hateful taunting laughter trailed behind me. When I came through the door crying Daddy Mac was sitting in his chair, shirtless, a cigarette in one hand, a beer in the other. He calmly listened and then gruffly commanded me to get back out there and stand up for myself. Fear roiled within me, but I would rather face the girls than disobey Daddy Mac.

Crying (because I always did when Daddy Mac chastised me and because my feelings were hurt) I marched back outside hoping they would be gone. They weren't. Honestly, I don't even remember what was said. They were probably making fun of my name: Ida. I remember they grabbed me—we wrestled—I stopped crying—we wrestled—they left. Regardless of who was victor, I felt a shift inside my eight-year-old heart. Daddy Mac had given me a lifelong gift: I was capable. I could stand up for myself. I could face fear. That would be the last time anyone bullied me.

I loved babies. My friends had babies in their homes, but mine was achingly absent of babies. When my best friend's mom had a baby, it was the definitive event of the year for me. It was better than my birthday, better than the Easter bunny, far better than Halloween, Thanksgiving was not even in the running, and almost as good as Christmas. The first of my three secret childhood wishes was birthed. I wanted a baby in my home. I wanted a brother or better yet, a new baby sister. I wanted a sibling.

The day finally came when little neighborhood visitors were allowed, and I followed my friend across the alley and into her building. She might be used to babies as her apartment was filled with brothers and sisters, but for me, it was a crowning moment. Her mother held a tiny bundle wrapped in a blanket the color of the evening sky at Grandma Lizzy's. I heard cooing and tender sighs and weak mewing. I had never seen a baby this new. I waited hand over mouth, eyes wide as the mother lay the wriggling, squirming baby onto the bed. She slowly unwrapped the blanket speaking mother-talk to the new little boy.

We were met with a smell wholly at odds with the sweet baby. We giggled and held our noses while the Mom proceeded to put on a fresh diaper. With an air of holding a superior poker hand my friend commented on her new brother's boy parts. She mistakenly believed I'd never seen a boy without his clothes since I had no brothers. She was obviously ignorant of the close proximity in which my family lived, and she was completely devoid of the knowledge that Daddy Mac never wore pajamas. Having played my full house, I stood smugly with my arms crossed and smiled. She chaffed a bit that I was neither surprised nor impressed with her disclosure.

However, her mother held the ace in the hole. She casually explained the procedure of the birds and bees to both her daughter and me. My friend was thunder-struck, but once again I held the winning hand. My royal flush success flaunted itself as I calmly replied I already knew that and walked out the door. "Who was the wise worldly one now?" my retreating back silently shouted.

The tears began before I reached the hall stairway. By the time I got to the alley, I was in full-fledged agony. I felt as if someone had reared back and let loose with a kick right in my center. I couldn't breathe. My friend's mother had taken something beautiful beyond words—babies-- and smeared it with the gagging stench of the goings-on-under-the-covers in the bed inches from my sleeping couch. The true revelation had not been the act itself, but that the act produced babies.

In addition to the secretive nighttime activities of the adults in my life, my birds-and-bees education had come together from various sources. Crude bar jokes. Drunken adult discussions. Porn in a box under the kitchen table. All I knew of making love came from the sordid side of life. It took years for the love and atoning sacrifice of Christ to reconcile that coarse and offensive act with beautiful innocent wonderful babies made with genuine love.

CHAPTER 8

"Names are the sweetest and most important sounds in any language". Dale Carnegie

Daddy Mac provided well for my mom and me. He had left Darby's and joined the Boilermaker union thus enabling us to move out of the city. During my fourth-grade year at nine years of age, Daddy Mac and Mama had saved enough to move to the big, wide, beautiful, tree-filled country.

    They bought a modest home on a few acres where the prairie meets the Missouri Ozarks. I learned self-sufficiency. Hunting, fishing, gardening, cooking, canning, sewing, and raising chickens, cows, pigs, and rabbits with the occasional raccoon, squirrel, and snake thrown in. I was an only child and entertained myself by taking care of my animals, building tree houses, and spending untold hours in the woods reading books and hunting. It was a solitary existence. I still wanted a little sister so I unconsciously morphed my love and attention to animals.

    One of the first things a child learns is her name.

    Mine was Ida. Oh, how I hated it. I hated the mere sound of it. It didn't fit me. It wasn't me. It sent chills, the bad kind, sliding down my neck onto my spine and exploding into my very soul every time someone said it.

IDA. It became a banner of mortification. This was exaggerated by childish immaturity but very real in my little world.

Fortunately for me, I didn't have to hear it at home, only at school. In Kansas City Kindergarten to fourth grade, I was called Ida. At home, I was Beth taken from my middle name Elizabeth which I adored. Elizabeth gave me warm fuzzies deluxe and sent my mind to wonder about the Queen whom Mama said was my namesake. I secretly wished everyone would call me Elizabeth, but I was too timid to ask.

And, then there was my last name, Ewing. I didn't think about it too much until just before we moved to the country. That's when I realized my mom's and dad's name was different from mine. Their name was McKee. I wondered about it but never asked. I kept silent about a lot of things.

After the move to the country upon enrolling me into my new one-room schoolhouse at Edmonson, which I thought was frightfully delightful, I didn't want my name to be different, I wanted my mama's name; I wanted Daddy Mac's name: McKee. The teacher said I had to use my real name, Ida Ewing on the school records, but, on a daily basis they could call me Beth McKee.

My heart was thrilled. A new school. A new name. A new start. I was euphoric.

The winter had a tight grip on the countryside, but I didn't care. The yard was covered in beautiful, white glistening-in-the-sun snow. It was a far cry from the gray, dirty trampled snow in the city. The trees were laden with snow and their limbs were draped in icicles. I still slept on a couch, but this one had a magical secret. It made into a bed. It wasn't a real bed, of course. And, it had a wide crack right down the middle. But if you slept to one side or the other it didn't matter. It was so much larger than I was used to. Daddy Mac thought I didn't need all that space, but Mama laid it flat for me anyway. I loved her for that.

As I helped Mama fold up the bedding and the couch, my heartbeat was so loud I feared I may not hear the school bus. I'd never ridden a bus. What if I missed it? What if I missed my first day at school? What if they kicked me out before I ever got to go? Mama and I were midway through folding the couch into a sitting position when I heard gravel crunching out in the road. I loved that sound. It was so much more friendly than city streets. It was like the rocks were speaking to me. Daddy Mac said the rocks came from a creek bed. I wondered if they missed the water.

The bus was coming! I dropped my side and the couch banged down flat again.

As I ran to the window I shouted, "Mama, Mama, it's here." She seemed excited for me and quickly helped me with my coat and handed me my brand-new lunch box--oh how I loved that little plaid lunch box. I ran out the door, my excitement overshadowing my shyness. The school bus was waiting at the end of the drive.

I wasn't too familiar with school buses having never ridden one, but even I knew this one was different. Way different. It was a dark blue station wagon. The driver smiled at me, got out, and opened the back door. "Good morning, Beth, isn't it?" I grinned from ear to ear. He called me Beth. Not Ida. Beth. This was going to be a great day.

I settled in the back seat and at the next stop, a football player got on. He was dressed in a numbered jersey, jeans, and a football helmet. When we got to school, the teacher insisted the football helmet come off. When it did it was a girl. Edmonson was full of surprises like that. I loved it.

We had one teacher for all grades first through eighth. They were a tight, loyal bunch of mixed girls and boys; I was accepted without prejudice.

I loved attending the cozy one-room schoolhouse at Edmonson, made good life-long friends, and grew up independent and curious, unafraid of dark nights, mysterious noises, and angry animals, yet shy with people.

Edmonson contributed to my happiness, despite living with frequent violent circumstances. In my innocence, I grew up thinking it was happiness that insulated me from a harsh and sometimes cruel environment but looking back I see it was really the Light of Christ. His Light shielded me from the worst in my life and implanted a life-long yearning for the knowledge and Love of God. The second of three secret wishes that lived in my heart was to go to church but Daddy Mac scoffed at religion and Mama seemed indifferent.

CHAPTER 9

> *"Wandering off the beaten path / You'll find a garden / In this garden you will find / A cobblestone path to a gnome home / In this gnome home you shall hear / Two gnomes stuck in a gnome drone Flailing their canes in the air Spilling gnome beer everywhere".*
> Sam DeRouen and Jacob DeRouen

The polar wind blew across our yard as if it had come straight from the arctic. But I didn't care. I inhaled the cold as if my life depended on it as if I had never breathed before. It was fresh and clean and crisp.

Since our move to the country, I had discovered the great outdoors. It provided peace, solitude, privacy, and as it turned out health. I stood beside the magnificent pine tree experiencing its resiny scent, fingering its soft needles when I heard footsteps crunching in the snow.

I turned to look and there before my very eyes stood a gnome. He stopped abruptly as startled to see me as I was to see him. He stood barely taller than I was, although he was stooped and scrunched which subtracted a portion of his height. He wore an old coat buttoned tight from chin to hem, gray from dye or age I couldn't tell which. His fedora of the same sad color and condition sat tilted atop his head, sweat-stained from humid Missouri summers gone by. His trousers flowed loosely down his legs and puddled atop dull brown boots that had trod these hills for decades.

His face was lined with years of living, his large ears seemed cocked waiting for me to speak. He leaned slightly toward me on his wooden cane, curious with tree rings and tiny knot holes. His gnarly hand grasped the cane as he planted it more firmly in the snow.

I was not afraid of this ancient gnome; I had encountered scarier men in the twilight zone of my parent's drinking establishments. He peered at me with twinkling eyes and asked through toothless gums was I the new folks. I replied in the affirmative and led him through the yard and into the house.

As he removed his coat, I saw sweat stains in the pits of its sleeves, it truly matched his hat then, and a pipe protruded from the inside pocket. The gnome introduced himself as Wilbur.

Wilbur turned out to be a neighbor and in every respect lived up to that description. His home was maybe three miles away in a beautiful little valley, or as Wilbur would say a "holler". His small cabin was hewn with logs from the surrounding forest, void of electricity or running water, and hosted a small wood-burning stove that squatted right in the middle of the single room. When its door stood ajar the smoldering coals inside looked like a beating heart. And I guess in a way it was.

Wilbur's yard was a showcase of his artistic endeavors. Garden gourds hollowed out and painted hung from low tree limbs serving as homes for generations of birds who came faithfully year after year to start their families. A tangle of dirt pathways lined with rocks painted in bright primary colors marked the way from the house to the outhouse, from the house to the garden, from the house, and up the hill to the main road. Upturned empty beer bottles decorated the ends of broken twigs on trees and stray wire poking up from his fence. Carved log benches sat on either side of what we now would call a firepit, but to Wilbur, it was a campfire.

For all the half-night and all-night parties that were thrown at my house, Daddy Mac never started a campfire. Perhaps he knew boozing and starting fires just didn't sync. Wilbur's campfire was always stone cold when I was there as if it was afraid to show me the sweet pleasures of childhood others enjoyed like soft acoustical music and blackened marshmallows squished into s'mores.

Wilbur walked everywhere, in every season. During summer he still wore old gray pants and without his coat, you could see they were hiked up and cinched tight with a brown belt made to fit his skinny frame with an extra hole punched in the leather. Oft times he opted for baling twine for a belt tied in multiple knots just to be sure it stayed in place.

The pants were pleated around his wiry waist making his pockets flare but still hanging heavy with tidbits picked up along the road. Bottlecaps, beer can pulls, and bug carcasses. Only Wilbur could make yard art out of shed locust skins.

Sometimes he and Daddy Mac pooled their beer can pulls; Wilbur's contribution was paltry next to the buckets full of beer tabs Daddy Mac collected on a regular basis. Mama joined the men and would sit for hours in the shade at the picnic table listening to country music twang and making long bracelets to string on the barbed and hog wire fence that enclosed our chicken yard. The Ozarks seem to spawn this homespun hometown bling.

When Daddy Mac was away on jobs, Wilbur was our go-to guy when things went awry. He wasn't too keen on plumbing emergencies but just let an animal get injured or a raccoon destroy a chicken house and all its inhabitants, and you could color him there.

One fine morning I stood under the redbud tree gazing through the entry hole of a birdhouse I had recently hung there. I wondered if the bluebird family had moved in yet. I could see what looked to be octagonal cells covering the doorway. At first, I thought it was a wasps' nest so before I yanked it out of there I wanted to be sure. The last thing I wanted was to destroy a bird's nest full of eggs. I stepped closer and stood on my tiptoes. I took hold of the birdhouse pulling it nearer to my eyes. Suddenly it all became crystal clear.

It was not part of the bird's nest. It was not wasps. It was the scaly underbelly of a snake. I shoved it away from me, screamed for Mama, and prayed the snake did not emerge from the swaying birdhouse. Mama immediately summed up the situation. Neither she nor I were adept at nor had any inclination to deal with snakes so there was only one solution. Wilbur.

My skinny little legs ran up the dusty road with purpose. I began calling his name as soon as I reached the top of his "holler". Wilbur responded immediately to the fear and urgency of my screaming. Without a word, he grabbed his walking stick and we started back toward my house as I began to tell the tale between gulping breaths of air. When he grasped the state of affairs and realized Mama was not somewhere unconscious and bleeding to death, his canter slowed to a normal gait that did not suggest a crazy person.

I was in the pattern of running ahead and then darting back to him just certain that at our current rate of speed the snake would surely get away. Finally, Wilbur said not to worry, the snake wasn't going anywhere. I slowed my pace, but my mind was racing to and from my house terrified of the fate of my little bluebirds.

When we reached our yard Mama was standing a respectable distance from the redbud tree, her arms crossed, her eyes glued to the birdhouse. It was as if she was willing that snake to stay put with her steely gaze. Wilbur conscripted a wire chicken catcher with a handy loop on the end for the task at hand. He proceeded to prod and push until it finally ensnared the snake's body. Then he gently pulled it out through the little bird door bringing the snake with it.

In today's world, I don't kill blacksnakes. We go to considerable lengths here on our farm to preserve their lives. But, in Mama's world, all snakes died. After all was said and done Wilbur strung it up in the redbud tree. The black snake stretched far above Wilbur's head with one end high in the branches and the other end dragging on the ground.

Folks passing by stopped for days just to have a look at it and say, " yep, that's a big un alright. Whatcha' gonna do with it?" Some wanted to make a belt or a hatband or just tan the hide for a trophy. Finally, Mama had had enough, and she commandeered Wilbur to sling it out into the woods across the road. After a few days, buzzards made short work of it.

When Daddy Mac returned from his work trip I had a tall tale to tell.

Wilbur continued his solitary life long after I married and left home. He walked the hills and lived in his little log house until one day a group of adolescent ruffians beat him to death thinking to get his treasure. The only treasure my little gnome ever had was his heart of gold.

CHAPTER 10

"No form of violence can ever be excused in a society that wishes to call itself decent."
Nelson Mandala

Daddy Mac was often a stern taskmaster, but in spite of it or because of it, I'm not sure which, he taught me some valuable lessons.

Daddy Mac and I didn't see eye to eye on most things, but even in my inexperienced and naive youthful heart, I knew it was the liquor speaking and acting most of the time. He loved his alcohol in any form. My parents consumed so much beer that the beer delivery truck stopped at our house. I thought that was normal. Weekends brought birds-of-a-feather friends who helped Mama and Daddy Mac consume case after case of beer. They stacked the cans pyramid-style on the kitchen table; the goal being to reach the ceiling.

By the time we moved to the country, I had tasted alcohol from every bottle and can. I knew the brand names of every beer, whiskey, and vodka. I hated the taste and smell of beer and whiskey, but my favorite liquor was peppermint schnapps. I outgrew the desire for peppermint in that form and by the time my age hit double digits I hated the sight, smell, or mention of any alcohol. I hated the change in Mama's eyes even after one beer and I hated the inebriated Daddy Mac. When liquor had its tentacles thoroughly entwined around Daddy Mac's will he blasphemed Christ. He often told illusory stories of Jesus getting drunk and laying in the gutter. It was tormenting for me. I put my hands over my ears and squeezed my eyes closed but it did not prevent the tears from flowing or the tight band of pain around my chest.

It was during times like these my mind wandered to that other daddy…the one on my birth certificate. The one named Frank Ewing. I loved Daddy Mac and I wanted him to love me, but when liquor fired his temper, I closed my eyes and my heart to him. During winter I went to the furthest corner of the tiny house to evade unpleasantness and in summer I escaped outside.

Nature welcomed me when I required refuge from the torrent of violence inside my house. My mind sought solace with Frank Ewing. If only he were alive. Mama had told me he had been killed in the war fighting for freedom. He was my private hero. If he were alive maybe, we could be a family. Maybe we would go to church. Maybe I could have a sister. Maybe he wouldn't drink. Maybe he wouldn't hit Mama.

In spite of Daddy Mac's rebellious lifestyle and willful malignment of Christ, when he wasn't drinking, I loved him, and I loved being with him. Someone had taught me two simple prayers, one for meals and one for bedtime. I cannot remember if it was Mama or Daddy Mac who took the time to teach me to pray, but my money's on Mama. The prayers were my go-to place for God. I said them my entire childhood. Every meal. Every night.

Before each meal, I was usually encouraged to ask the blessing on the food, especially if we had company, which was frequent. One time I opened my mouth to pray, and the words did not come to mind. I panicked. My face burned; my eyes stung. I opened my eyes and Daddy Mac was looking at me across "THE TABLE". This was no ordinary table. This was the seat of power. This was home base, a stronghold for every decision made, a bastion for every argument waged. The Table where meals were shared. The Table was the only place a family prayer was ever spoken.

I sheepishly said, "I forgot." His mouth crooked into a parody of a smile and said, "No you didn't." His look and tone implied I had purposefully not said the prayer and that I had lied. My humiliation was complete.

Mama's eighth-grade education always shamed her, but she was proud of Daddy Mac. He graduated high school and excelled both scholastically and in sports. He was a hell-raiser even then. His mother, Grandma Lizzy, told me he always sought out trouble and ignored the consequences. One time while he was still a small boy, he so provoked her she beat his head against the little sidewalk that ran in front of the house to the barn. I can't imagine it was too hard, but Grandma felt guilty for the rest of her life.

Because Daddy Mac had done well in school I always strived for good grades. Because he was in sports, I would play sports. Daddy Mac loved to sing, so I would join the choir. He had toured with country music star Hank Thompson in 1948 before Hank's career really took off. Daddy Mac was proud of his association with Hank. They had both served in the Navy, they were both rabble-rousers, they loved to sing, drink, smoke, enjoyed the company of women, and shared a middle name--William.

Daddy Mac loved to tell the story when Hank wrote "Green Light". They were in a car stopped at a red traffic light when Hank burst into song making up the lyrics and tune as they sat waiting for the light to turn. "Green Light" was Hank's third hit song topping out at number seven on the US Country music chart. Daddy Mac was part of the foundation that helped Hank Thompson become a star.

When Hank's music played over the radio it always spawned Daddy Mac's nostalgic moments. He would get out his guitar, sing "Green Light" and retell the story of Hank Thompson's rise to fame. Daddy Mac toured with Hank during the same time the "Brazos Valley Boys" got their start. Their claim to fame was adding that famous "swing" sound to country music and went on to popularize that arrangement. They are still performing today with members who inherited the best western swing band in the country and who played and sang with the golden voice of Hank Thompson.

I never knew if Daddy Mac sang with Hank's band the "Brazos Valley Boys" or not, but it never mattered to me. Some of our best times as a family were when Daddy Mac played guitar and sang to Mama and me. One of my favorite songs was "Green Grass Grew All Around". It was a silly ditty that we sang over and over. Every time Daddy Mac's guitar came out of the case I requested "Green Grass Grew All Around". I sing it to this day. We all loved music. It was one of our few common bonds.

Daddy Mac instilled in me the love of dancing. At an early age he whirled around the dance floor holding me tight. When I was a little older, he placed me on his feet and off we went waltzing or two-stepping to someone's country music hit on the jukebox. In every bar we were ever in, we danced. If there was no dance floor, he made one by clearing and rearranging tables. The proprietors never minded and even if they did Daddy Mac was a force to be reckoned with.

Daddy Mac was a challenging paradox of contradictions. He could be jovial, friendly, and even loving in a hands-off kind of way. Or he could splay you wide, deep, and doggedly with sarcasm and malicious intent. And, worst of all, he could backhand you, punch you in the gut or blacken your eye. He never physically abused me, but Mama and his friends were well acquainted with his mistreatments. His mood usually depended on how much Jack Daniels, Falstaff or Sloe Gin coursed through his system.

He could be generous to a fault with those truly in need. They had only to ask, and Daddy Mac forked over whatever was requested, money, food, lumber, even liquor. Occasionally, unsavory fair-weather friends took advantage of his generosity, but it didn't seem to stop him from continuing to be the go-to guy for assistance when folks were beset with trials. Daddy Mac wasn't fond of giving physical help such as moving, haying, doing chores, or cleaning out a chicken house but just present a doctor's bill and his money was forthcoming.

Daddy Mac's moods ranged from vile and vulgar verbal abuse to violent physical altercations. Occasionally, pistols came into play.

Daddy Mac was a boilermaker through and through. It was hard demanding dirty work and required him to travel several months of the year. Usually, he was gone Spring thru Fall and tried to take the winter off. During one of his absences, some friends invited Mama to the local bar to have a few. To my knowledge, this was the only occasion Mama ever went to a bar without him. I was playing in the gravel parking lot out front and thought I saw Daddy Mac drive by but decided it couldn't have been him.

Later that night our friends dropped Mama and me off at home and sure enough, Daddy Mac was there. He was in a raging temper because Mama hadn't been home when he arrived. Mama did not have a driver's license and even if she did, we only had one vehicle which Daddy Mac had taken to work, so she was *always* at home.

At first Daddy Mac just yelled and cussed because he had come home to an empty house. But as the evening wore on and the liquor flowed, he became increasingly violent. We often had a variety of guests of sorts who stayed in our unattached garage on a sleeping cot. We had one at that time, but he was silent and uninvolved. He sat on one end of the sofa with Daddy Mac on the other end.

I had a sweet little blue parakeet named Perky whose cage for some reason was sitting midway in front of the sofa.

Mama was sitting in an overstuffed chair directly across from the sofa; I perched on the chair's arm. Mama was crying. I was crying. Daddy Mac was swearing and yelling. The white-faced friend was silent.

Perky alternated between huddling in freight on the floor of his cage and flying manically to the top of his cage, then jumping once more to the cage floor. I've often wondered why I didn't cover his cage with a towel to calm him down.

I was about ten years old and accustomed to drunken brawls, but this one seemed different. From the very beginning when we drove into the driveway and realized Daddy Mac was home, fear took hold of me.

Daddy Mac was a jealous man. I had seen that play out numerous times in physical abuse episodes with my mother. I instinctively knew this time was going to be worse.

Mama got up from the chair and walked across the small living room to Daddy Mac. She stood in front of him trying to calm his temper. Trying to soothe the raging bull. It didn't work, of course. Daddy Mac grabbed her and pulled her down between him and our guest on the couch simultaneously knocking over the birdcage stand. Our friend caught the cage with the terrified squawking parakeet; birdseed and water splattered across the living room floor. Daddy Mac pulled his pistol, cocked it, and put it to Mama's temple. She screamed. I screamed. Perky screamed.

Horror swept across me. I'd witnessed many brawls in my short life and nursed my mother's bruises with child-like concern. I ignored violence by packing it away in the secret box in my heart, but this, this was new. This could be life-changing, and life-taking. My mouth turned to sand; my voice was lost in the turmoil of my emotions.

I sat frozen on the arm of the chair watching the scene play out; Daddy Mac cursing, demanding, threatening. Mama weeping. At one moment she was begging, the next she was defiant. Mama was scrappy like that even in the face of death.

Mama normally put nights of physical abuse behind her by the time the next day arrived, forgiveness an unspoken presence. She was never fawning or sycophantic; she just went on with business as usual. But this time it took a little longer. By the next afternoon, Mama was still silent during Daddy Mac's strained attempts at conversation. I don't know if this shored me up with courage, or if after years of violence my little soul had just had enough.

Daddy Mac had jovially loaded us all into the farm truck along with fishing rods, bait, and assorted paraphernalia designed to outsmart the local crappie. The Osage River was just a couple of miles from our house, so we headed to Hunts Cove, one of our favorite fishing holes.

We bounced along the eroded and rough gravel road toward the water. Daddy Mac, having finally had his fill of our silence, began to berate Mama. I sat between them. Something began to stir within me. Hot and agitating. Years of unrecognized hurt and anger had settled deep inside me and without warning, it erupted. I blurted, "I wish you would just go down below and stay there." I would never have said the obvious word.

I never sassed Daddy Mac. I never argued or pleaded my case or tried to negotiate. I always took his punishment and judgment without any visible response except perhaps a silent tear or two. We were all shocked at my outburst, me most of all.

He slammed on the brakes, throwing us all forward as we sat on the bench seat. The old truck sputtered and died. Fishing gear slid across the truck bed in the back. The can of worms tipped over. Sunlight streamed through the windshield; dust motes floated mindlessly across the beams. I couldn't believe I had spoken. Surely those words had not come from me. My mouth felt dry; my heart raced.

Daddy Mac slammed his foot down on the clutch, turned the key, and started the engine. His fist clenched the gear shift knob protruding from the floor just inches from my knee. I dare not look at him. Silence lay thick in the truck like a suffocating blanket. He turned the steering wheel, jammed the truck into gear, and jerked forward. Then backward. Then forward. When he succeeded in turning the truck around, he took us home bouncing and bobbing down the narrow pitted road without a word.

Daddy Mac retreated to The Table with a can of beer and a cigarette. Mama and I escaped outdoors. She didn't scold or shout. She didn't defend or justify or rationalize. She didn't cry or rant or rage. She simply said, "You must apologize."

The anger within me had been replaced with first fear of Daddy Mac, then horror at what I had done, and finally remorse. Later that day I told him I was sorry and the whole sorry episode was never mentioned again.

A miracle happened that horrible night. Something reached through the shroud of wrath and jealousy and prompted Daddy Mac to put down the gun. I always thought it was God. Daddy Mac was not a church-going person and he thought those who went were the worst kind of hypocrite. But, in my limited understanding of Heavenly workings, I knew in my heart of hearts that God had been involved in cooling Daddy Mac's temper and sparing Mama's life.

And I didn't know it at the time, but He saved me, too. Not only physically, but mentally, emotionally, and spiritually. From that moment on, God was a real Presence to me. A Presence and a Protector. He was my Father in Heaven. He loved me, and I loved Him.

A year or so after the gun incident Mama took me to church. It was the first and only time. I always wanted to go–after all, attending church was my second secret wish. I pestered her until she finally gave in. The small country church sat on a picturesque hill just up from the river and a couple of miles from us. It was created from beautiful native stone, just like our house.

The congregants met every other Wednesday night, never on Sunday, as they had what Daddy Mac called a traveling preacher. Wednesday was good because Daddy Mac was out of town working; on Sunday he would be home and Mama would never have consented to take me.

I was overjoyed. Excitement sparked throughout my mind, and it seemed impossible to sit still. I was not even aware the word reverent existed. When it came time for the children to separate from the adults, I got up and ran across the chapel. Of course, I was the only one running and Mama was mortified. After we left and Mama explained proper behavior in a church did not include bounding across the room like a wild untamed deer, I understood her embarrassment. Mama and I never returned to this little church for worship, but we would both be back for a funeral and a wedding.

"Now I lay me down to sleep; I pray the Lord my soul to keep. If I should die before I wake; I pray the Lord, my soul, to take." Lay Monk Preston 1700's

After some persuasion from the local general store owner at Edmonson who also started a little bible-believing church, Daddy Mac consented to let me go to summer Bible School that was held at the Edmonson schoolhouse. I was thrilled. That's where I met Jesus. That's where I gave Him my heart forever. I had always said my two little prayers at the appropriate times, one for meals and one for bedtime, but this is where I learned I could pray in every place, and I could share anything that was in my heart with Him. And I learned He was with me. Anytime, anywhere, always.

I attended the Bible School several summers relishing in the company of other believers. There was a big baptismal ceremony on the last day of Bible School. I fiercely wanted to be baptized, to show Jesus I belonged to Him, but Daddy Mac refused. My disappointment was palpable. I would be an adult before that dream came true as part of my secret wish number two.

CHAPTER 11

"There is a passion for hunting something deeply implanted in the human breast."
Charles Dickens

We were hunters. And fishers and woodsmen and animal lovers. I didn't realize I was a Tomboy until we moved to the Ozarks. In the city, I loved dresses and mirrors and ruffled white anklets. I always wore my hair long and Mama spent time brushing it every day. In the country I wore jeans, and boots, carelessly threw my hair into a ponytail, and carried a gun from a very young age.

By the time I was twelve, I hunted squirrels and rabbits by myself and regularly won turkey shoots against older more experienced hunters. Harry's Place, the local country bar, sponsored a couple of shoots a year. Well before the contest began the men were throwing back beer in the tavern. Daddy Mac loved bragging about how well his kid could shoot and I suspect there was betting involved. Most of the men took their loss to me in stride, but there were a few who took issue. As Daddy Mac and Harry used to say to them, "Don't go away mad, just go away."

Daddy Mac wanted a boy; I tried to give him one, but he still insisted my hair be long. In my heart, I wanted to be daddy's little girl although I didn't know that descriptive at the time. Every time I wrote my name--Beth McKee—on a school paper I felt good. I felt included. I belonged to Daddy Mac. I was his little girl. But my heart knew I wasn't. My heart knew my secret. I was still Ida Ewing.

As a family, we hunted at all hours: mornings for squirrels, afternoons for mushrooms, nights for raccoons. We fished in the summer and hunted rabbits in the winter. We filled washtubs full of crappies, feed sacks full of rabbits, and gunnie sacks full of raccoons. I carried the gunny sack. The hunting party usually consisted of Daddy Mac, some of his friends, and me. Mama went some of the time, but mostly it was me and the men.

Daddy Mac taught me to skin a raccoon, flesh out the hide, and cure it on a stretching board. It was a laborious task, but I loved it. Daddy Mac took pride in cutting the tree, milling the lumber at his sawmill, and hewing it into the perfect stretching board. We had various sizes of skins from assorted animals: raccoons, possums, coyotes, fox, and squirrels. I always thought a skunk's thick and luxurious fur would be beautiful, but Daddy Mac never agreed.

Regardless of the work I did, whether it was raising calves, pigs, goats, chickens, and ducks or selling animal furs Daddy Mac always shared the revenue with me. I never had a normal children's job like babysitting but I never lacked money in my piggy bank.

Spoon-bill season took fishing to a whole new level. Spring always brought a fresh enthusiasm that had lain dormant all winter. It stirred the hunter's blood to slay the dragon drawing forth the latent predator in every man.

Warm breezes and bright blue skies witnessed the area's greatest public spectacle of the year, not only fishermen, but audiences of all ages come to cheer and observe their champions lay waste the prey. Prehistoric Polyodon spathula pit against primitive man wielding spears.

The great paddlefish of the Osage River traces back to over 125 million years ago—nearly two times older than the celebrated Tyrannosaurus Rex and is the only member of its family still living on planet earth. [i] They emerge from the deep dark murky waters of the river bottom once a year to ensure the continuance of their species. They come to spawn. [ii]

The killing season was short; one had to be ready. Daddy Mac began his preparation early and proceeded carefully. His waders, still stiff from winter temps, were brought in from the storage shed. He meticulously inspected every inch for holes or tears. He cleaned off every spec of grit and grime. He lovingly hung them to "fall out" naturally as they warmed to the ambient temperature of the room waiting for the paddlefish predator to step in.

Daddy Mac's hunting closet housed his many guns, various calibers and rounds of ammunition, a wide assortment of knives, weapon cleaning utensils and products, and his one and only paddlefish harpoon. He sharpened it with the keen eye of a hunter. The gaff glistened with lethal intent.

The anticipated spoonbill season had arrived. Daddy Mac's daily ritual singing of "Oh What A Beautiful Morning" echoed through the early morning mist. We were up well before dawn and having packed the gear the night before we used the time to eat a small breakfast. Didn't want to be bogged down with stuffed gullets or need the restroom in the midst of the harvest.

Daddy Mac, Mama, and I loaded into the old truck and headed out for the five-minute drive to the cove. We were by far not the first ones to arrive. Overnight camping was frowned upon but forgiven for those whose drive was considerably longer than ours.

Daddy Mac donned his waders, picked up his harpoon, and started for the water. The gravel lost its crunch on the muddy surface as he walked resolutely toward the water's edge. The other fisherman sported a variety of costumes ranging from high-end rubber waders complete with matching jacket, hat, and a stainless-steel gaff to those barefoot souls with fewer resources and rolled-up overalls, patched plaid shirts, and a knife duct-taped to a long pole cut the day before in the woods. No matter the income strata all the fishermen were high on enthusiasm and confidence.

The hunters stood silently thigh-deep in the murky water spaced several feet from one another. Although it was too dark to see clearly, their eyes scanned the water's calm surface; their weapons still and poised to strike. The air was still as if it, too, waited. Mama and I stood on the shore barely breathing along with the other observers mutely supporting their fishers.

I love that time just before sunrise. It's as if the earth is so tired of night, that she gets ahead of herself and allows the faintest soft inkling of light before the sun pops over the horizon. Suddenly, vision cleared; the fisherman's senses soared. Simultaneously across the cove scores of people in and out of the water witnessed a miracle of nature.

The paddlefish were here! The water roiled and churned with prehistoric parents. They were on the surface, below the surface occasionally breaching above the surface. Spectators cheered and screamed; fishers struck and stabbed and swore.

I climbed up into the bed of the truck to better my view. Some were already coming out of the water dragging their trophy behind, blood trailing like a chilling marker of death. Daddy Mac was still out there. He waded deeper into the water, eyes focused, mind concentrated. A shadow passed beside him and instantly Daddy Mac thrust his gaff into the water. He let out a loud and long yell—a warrior's cry of conquest. By the time he wrangled it to the truck his waders were covered with blood, and pink smears slashed his face beside the grin of victory. Strictly speaking, I wouldn't have cared if he hadn't caught a thing. For me, it was the thrill of it all and being able to be a part of Daddy Mac's world.

Spoonbill gigging was one of the things I never tried. Right up there with catfish noodling. I just didn't have the body weight or strength for it. But I was right there beside Daddy Mac when the men in the black of night, held their breath, ducked beneath the water's surface, shoved their arms into a catfish hole, grabbed the fish by the jaws and gills, dragged them out fighting, biting, and splashing, then hit them in the head with a rock to finish the kill.

One of my favorite adventures was frogging. We frequented neighborhood ponds with and without farmer permission at the midnight hour. Armed with gunny sacks, flashlights, gigging poles, and beer we set out to fulfill our quest.

The trick was to shine the flashlight along the banks and shallows until two pinpricks of fluorescence looked back at you. Then, you stealthily, silently crept toward the eyes keeping the beam centered on the frog so he remained blinded by the light. Then you swiftly jab and stab until the frog dangles lifelessly at the end of your pole. The frog is then crammed into the gunny sack which guess who is carrying.

I loved to run along the banks of the ponds trying to keep my footing on the wet grass. Occasionally I slipped into a fall, landed on my bottom, and could feel a snake slither out from beneath me. Considering the amount of time I spent in nature, day and night, it was a miracle I was never bitten by a snake. I now believe the good Lord's angels worked overtime to keep me safe.

When the gunny sacks were full or when the men could no longer resist the thought of fried frog legs, we headed home.

The makeshift portable skinning-cleaning-gutting table is retrieved from the storage shed—an old door and two sawhorses—and reassembled under a tree beside the barnyard fence. Me with my flashlight served as the light pole albeit somewhat more unstable but considerably more engaged. Animal guts never bothered me unless the animal had been born and/or lovingly raised in my barn.

While Daddy Mac and I and whatever friends happened to be along on this particular anuran amphibian escapade were readying the frogs for the next step in their culinary journey, Mama was heating up the lard in cast iron skillets. By this time, it was one or two in the morning, no matter. Our household was not governed by something as immaterial and inconsequential as a clock.

Someone took over light pole duty as I carried a small white enamel dishpan full to the brim with clean, wet, naked frogs into the kitchen. The frogs had been dissected so that only a portion of the backs and all the plump meaty legs remained. Mama was ready with a pan full of flour, spices, salt, and pepper for coating the frogs then gently immersed them into the hot grease.

I stood expectantly beside the stove waiting for my favorite part of the entire evening. I was not disappointed. The frog legs began twitching and jerking, literally dancing in the skillet. Country music blared from the tiny radio on The Table as if in accompaniment. I gleefully clapped my hands as I watched their performance; sometimes

Mama also danced a jig, but most often she was all business and would shoo me out the door for another load of frog legs from the skinners.

Alcohol enhanced and embellished upon stories of frogs actually jumping out of the skillet, but I never witnessed that. Daddy Mac always said it was the hot grease but in reality, the phenomenon is caused by the sodium in salt triggering a biochemical reaction in the frog's muscle.

"Any man can help make a child, but it takes a special man to help raise a child."
Tony Gaskins

We lived and breathed fish. Mama baked, dried, fried, froze, and canned fish. We sauteed, fricasseed, smoked, and grilled fish. Fishing was a recreation, a hobby, and a food storage staple. We fished with poles from the bank, trolled in boats in the coves, sat trotlines in the river, sunk traps in the shallows, dispatched long lines in the deep currents, and noodled the undersides of low water bridges.

I had caught every kind of fish available in the Ozarks. Some were, according to Daddy Mac, just trash fish, like Carp and Needle Nose Gar. Some were the in-between-fundamental fish, like Crappie and Sunfish which we caught by the washtubs full. And others were the trophy fish like Rainbow trout and Wide-mouth bass.

Daddy Mac had taught me you don't just decide to throw a line in the water. Whether you're catching fish or hunting deer it takes forethought, planning, and a six-pack. On this particular autumn morning, our prey was Channel Catfish.

Catching the Channel cats was an art. The catfish year was divvied into three parts: pre-spawn, spawn and post-spawn. Then you overlayed that info with seasons, temperature, and habitat. You throw in a lucky fishing cap, an expertly constructed trotline, and properly seasoned bait. The most important, most essential, most indispensable component of trot lining for the big gray cats was the bait.

The bait took weeks of preparation and Daddy Mac had his special recipe. First, one acquired fresh chicken livers which worked out better if the timing coincided with Mama's menu of chicken and dumplings since there would be an ample supply of newly butchered fowl. The chicken livers were placed in a clean gallon empty Armour lard bucket. Along with the livers, as much fresh blood as possible was added to the mix.

After the lid was securely placed on the revolting concoction it was put on top of the cistern where the sun beat unrestrained. Gasses built up in the container causing the lid and sides to bulge, so the next day and each day thereafter the container needed to be vented. If one failed in this duty, unspeakable results were the consequence. I speak from experience. If you've never encountered rotten chicken livers sprayed on and covering all adjacent surfaces, consider yourself blessed. Since the cistern was directly out our back door, Daddy Mac did not take kindly to my errant behavior in regard to venting the bait. Once it blew, the stench remained for days and true to its name it baited dogs, cats, possums, and blowflies. Even the carrion-eating vultures circled the house in confused unfulfilled anticipation.

After several days to a couple of weeks—depending on the weather—of this procedure the revolting recipe was ready for the next step. Mama hated the next step. The recipe needed a binding agent so the concoction could be rolled into balls.

Daddy Mac measured some flour or sometimes cornmeal out of Mama's canisters and took the ripe lard can out into the chicken yard as far away from the house as he deemed necessary but still not far enough for Mama. She would never be involved in the mixing as her very active gag reflex prevented any actual work from being done. Daddy Mac used a large tree stump a.k.a chicken-killing block as a table and poured the flour into the rotten chicken livers. He had a large old spoon that had been specifically designated for making bait and barred from the kitchen.

At this juncture, the recipe allowed a certain amount of creativity and leeway. Daddy Mac could add whatever was on hand that would add to the putrid, penetrating, and pungent mixture. Sardines (which was inexplicably the only fish Grandma Lizzy would eat), cut-up inedible fish parts from last week's catch, or any other despicable, indescribable ingredient that would make the aptly named Stink Bait stink. Catfish in general love stink.

Daddy Mac dutifully rolled small amounts of the bait between his palms making small bait balls, stink vaporizing off him in odoriferous waves. He proudly lined them up on the tree stump like little soldiers fresh from a latrine lagoon. He left them out to dry for several hours, then my job came up in the queue. I had an empty bread sack on each hand—plastic gloves not yet being in supply—scooped up the bait balls and deposited them into a third plastic bag. I discarded the bag gloves, grabbed a twist tie, and closed up the bait bag. Depending on the scope of the fishing trip, sometimes we had one or multiple bags full of bait. I then put them in an empty metal minnow bucket, put on the lid, and stowed the whole malodourous mess in the storage shed to wait for the big day.

The mechanism for dispensing the Stink Bait is a trotline. Trotlines consist of a long heavy nylon cord called the mainline. The mainline could be as long as a fisherman's aspiration. Drop lines made from smaller-diameter nylon cord cut into 15-to-18-inch lengths were attached at regular intervals to the mainline with a swivel. A hook was then fastened to the end of the drop line with another swivel. The swivels help to keep the lines from becoming hopelessly entangled, a predicament not always avoidable. Other short lines were cut and attached to the mainline at longer intervals to hold the bobbers. A bobber is a floating device that holds the mainline off the bottom of the river. We used anything we could close securely enough to make it float for a bobber, various kinds of cans, and jugs. Every once in a while, Daddy Mac would insist on using an empty gallon glass whiskey jug just for fun. Yes, he had empty gallon-size whiskey jugs.

The miscellany of bobbers was cached in the ubiquitous gunny sack. Our trotline had been prepared and was neatly rolled onto a board. Our Stink Bait was successfully reeking. Daddy Mac, a fisherman friend of his, and I loaded our gear and ourselves into the old truck. I sat in the bed of the truck with the bait. We bumped, jumped, and jolted down the gravel road to the river, the boat bouncing along behind.

There are several ways to execute trot lining. Our favorite procedure was to secure the line to something on the bank, preferably a tree or tree root then extend the length of the cord into the water tying a large rock at the other end for an anchor.

We piled into the boat. Daddy Mac was the navigator, captain, and foreman so he sat in the stern by the outboard motor. His friend sat at the bow of the boat and took direction from the captain. I sat in the middle of the boat by the bait.

We had everything we needed for the next phase of trotline fishing except an anchor. There was no shortage of rocks on the Ozark River shore. Any size, any shape. Daddy Mac called out instructions describing exactly what sort of rock he wanted. His friend picked up and discarded one after the other frustration mounting at both ends of the boat.

At last, they both simultaneously spied the perfect specimen. Daddy Mac maneuvered the boat closer, his friend grumping about how he hoped this was the "perfect" rock reached over and secured it between his hands, raised it up to eye level, and turned around so Daddy Mac could inspect and approve.

The rock was inches away from my face. My eyes fastened on a large cotton-mouth water moccasin all three feet of him woven and spiraled in and around the various cavities of the rock. His head and neck extended several inches from his hole. Our eyes locked and both our mouths opened.

The trademark white interior of his mouth glistened in the bright sun. I could see his fangs, delicate harbingers of death rising in response to danger. I could hear his warning hiss overlay the gentle lapping of the water against the boat. Fear froze me to my seat. I couldn't even scream.

Unaware of the snake, our friend continued his conversation about whether Daddy Mac thought the rock suitable for our purpose. Daddy Mac stood up in the boat—an absolute no-no—yelled obscenities at the snake, the rock, and his friend. After several moments of confusion, it began to dawn upon the rock bearer that something was amiss. He turned the rock just enough to see the snake's protruding, angry, hissing head then threw it with the unnatural strength of the horrified several yards out into the river. The impact of the splashdown mimicked the Freedom 7 that would happen four years later.

We all three worked diligently and quickly to mold a wad of stink bait around each hook as the line was lowered into the water carefully and with great anticipation. The trotline was eventually set; the bobbers bobbing softly in the current. Sometimes we left the line and returned the next day. Sometimes we waited on the shore armed with binoculars watching the jugs for any activity. If the jug bobbed intermittently, we knew it was probably a small Channel cat. If it thrashed about in a frenzy, we had a big one! Most of the catfish were about two to three feet in length and were voracious fighters. The biggest one was on the last deepest hook on the trotline and was almost as long as I was tall. Daddy Mac's goal was to catch one over a hundred pounds, but that was the one that got away.

Sometimes just to mix it up a bit, Daddy Mac decided we'd try for the great Flathead Catfish. The Flathead is the only catfish that doesn't go for Stink bait regardless of how tempting the smell. His predator instincts drive him to relish the kill therefore only live bait will lure him to the hook. I loved it when we fished for Flatheads because Daddy Mac only used the one live bait guaranteed to get the big elusive catfish into the pan: goldfish. Many states outlaw the use of goldfish as bait, but Missouri never has. Even if it had I'm quite sure it would not have deterred Daddy Mac.

The slippery shiny tiny golden fish never failed to draw my attention. I could spend hours playing with them and I usually managed to finagle a few to keep in a bowl at home. Since we had moved to the country our trips to Grandma Lizzy's farm had diminished. But if I had goldfish on hand, I would take them to Grandpa Henry's to put in the beloved little magical pond in their front yard.

Today I am neither hunter nor fisherman. But, the many days and nights I spent with Daddy Mac in pursuit of game afforded me a kind of peculiar education I couldn't have learned in any other way.

CHAPTER 12

> *"Was it more obscene to say it, to write it, or to set it in type? On the breath it could be taken by a breeze or crowded out by chatter; it could be misheard or ignored. On the page it was a real thing. It had been caught and pinned to a board, its letters spread in a particular way so that anyone who saw it would know what it was."*
> Pip Williams, <u>The Dictionary of Lost Words</u>

Daddy Mac never got sick. Mama had regular bouts with the flu and other maladies, but Daddy Mac was robust, rowdy, and randy almost to the end. He had no sympathy for anyone who did get sick. The cramped living quarters and lack of green space in the city contributed to my annual visits to the children's hospital. Mama blamed my frequent illnesses on her aunt, and that long ago attempt to let the harsh Colorado climate claim my life.

Living in the city, I had been sickly and anemic. Pneumonia claimed me every winter and I was no stranger to "croup tents" in the hospital. But, when I began spending my time outdoors, summer and winter, when we began to eat off the "land"—hunting, fishing, gardening, my body not only adjusted to the lifestyle changes, it thrived. The crisp clean country air beckoned me out of the smoke-filled rooms into the forest. Daddy Mac and Mama were both chain-smokers; a habit that would eventually take Mama's life.

On the slim occasion, I did get sick, I didn't stay down long. Our small house was a vast improvement over the tiny apartment in the city, but it still only had three main rooms: a bedroom, a living room, and a kitchen. The bathroom was a joy; a far cry from the community bathroom of the past.

I had slept on the couch my entire life, and even though we had a new house, I still slept on the couch. So, when I was sick, my sick bed was right in the middle of all the action: adults gathered around The Table, drinking, smoking, swearing, and swapping tall tales. Daddy Mac couldn't abide my idleness no matter if it was caused by illness. Ironically, it instilled in me a good work ethic accompanied by a determination to work through sickness with grit and fortitude accompanied by a generous dose of guilt for being sick in the first place.

Mama and Daddy Mac's child-rearing skills may have been suspect by my teachers and friends' parents, but they had their own parenting style. Even though they lifted small things like ashtrays from bars and corn from the neighbor's field, they insisted on my adherence to the do-not-steal rule. Once I pilfered some caps from a store for my prized pistola and Mama made me take them back. I was seldom ever in a store except for the grocery store, so the wide world of goods offered on display was tempting beyond my ability to resist. Taking those caps back to the store embarrassed me to my core and made a lasting impression. I never stole anything again even to the point of a paper clip from an employer.

No one could swear like Daddy Mac, but Mama's tongue was loosed when she was drinking, and she could match him and any of his friends word for word. So, the repertoire of blue language I learned from day one lay at the ready when the occasions called for emphasis. I only remember three of those occasions.

The first was at the local bar before we moved from the city. I learned a new word. I'm quite sure, considering my environment, I had heard it before but somehow it had never caught my attention. In the small confines of that smoky little bar, it seemed as if the word flew out of someone's mouth, glided through the air, slipped into my ears, and stuck in my brain.

It circled round and round, repeating itself. I wandered outside the bar and sat on the curb under the streetlight. I loved words even then and knew how to sound them out to arrive at an approximate spelling. I found a small rock in the gutter (how appropriate) and discovered that it worked for makeshift chalk. I began practicing my best second-grade penmanship on the sidewalk.

I sounded out the word and wrote: F *** U *** K on the rough cement. Then I wrote it again. And, again. AND AGAIN, until the entire section of the sidewalk was covered with my new word. When there was no more room, I tried to fill the sky with it. I shouted it over and over until I was sure it had reached the stars.

Bar patrons coming and going smiled and laughed at my antics. I didn't care. I had a new word. Words are powerful. More powerful than we realize. Words create. Words destroy. Words inspire. Words discourage.

I began to notice the word everywhere in every discourse in every situation spoken by children and adults. Why hadn't I heard it before? It was pervasive. I also noticed it accompanied anger, violence, drunkenness, insolence, vulgarity, and rudeness of every kind. As time went by I came to hate my new word. I loathed the sound of it. I cringed and shied away every time it was spoken. Its very utterance conjured ugly situations and abhorrent memories.

As I grew older, I deliberately put myself out of reach of that word by associating with folks who never said it. Later in my life, I could go days, weeks, and months without so much as a whisper of that word.

Then, as an adult, I'm not really sure when it happened, but the word crept slowly back into my life. I noticed it being said in casual conversation by folks who didn't spend all their free time in a bar. I heard it in the business world at work where it was once taboo to use profanity. I heard it spoken by teens, pre-teens and gasp, elementary children and double-gasp, teachers. I heard it at the gas station, the grocery store, on the escalator, on the television, and at the movies. It was everywhere. And each time I heard it, I cringed inside. I still do.

The second encounter with my participation in bad language came in the graveled parking lot of the neighborhood country bar, Harry's Place. After hours of entertaining myself, I took a rock and wrote an expletive on the side of our new car. This was the second time a small chalk-like rock was my unwitting accomplice in learning and practicing the art of swearing.

It was the only new car we ever had and was a source of pride with my folks. Of course, the dust on the car from our gravel roads was a perfect canvas for my proud display of penmanship and readily noticeable to Daddy Mac. He took one look at the word scratched across the side of his car and said the very word he saw. It started with a mere whisper and with each repetition became louder and louder until at last he flew into a tirade about the worthlessness of the local boys, how they would never amount to anything and had no respect for another person's property.

I stood wide-eyed and silent beside him; I did not correct him. The faint undertaking of my folly was noticeable on the door's blue paint until the day we sold the car.

My last childhood experience with alternative gutter language came about abruptly with the force of a slap across my face. Some unremembered event caused me to react with a quick and very loud very common expletive. In fact, it was the very word I had scrawled across the door of our new Edsel many years before. I don't remember the catalyst for my outburst, but the result is still emblazoned in my mind. No sooner had the word escaped my mouth than Mama drew back her hand and slapped me. I think it shocked her as much as it did me. As if by unspoken consent, she never hit me again and I never swore again.

CHAPTER 13

" Hope is the thing with feathers.
That perches in the soul,
And sings the tune without the words,
And never stops at all."
Emily Dickinson

Of course, I dearly loved my Mama. I mean, she was my mama. We had our special times together when Daddy Mac went on jobs. Being a boilermaker for the union, he traveled on jobs all around our four-state area. Mostly, he worked in the summer. Since I was out of school during summers, that meant Mama and I had three months to ourselves punctuated by Daddy Mac's occasional foray home for a weekend, which was rare.

When we still lived in the city, Mama and I went by train to visit Daddy on a job. It was the first and only time. I'm pretty sure our policy of not visiting Daddy had something to do with a young woman who, even to my child's way of thinking, seemed too chummy with Daddy Mac, and he with her.

As I stated before, Daddy Mac was notoriously jealous, and frequently played out his suspicions with physical abuse on Mama. Perhaps his own conscience was at play here.

Daddy Mac only hit me once. I was in kindergarten, and he spanked me with a belt which to this day I feel was totally deserved. I'm a quick learner and never had corporal punishment again. Despite his shortcomings, I totally loved him. I wanted to be Daddy's little girl.

Shortly after moving to the country and the whole what-name-am-I-going-by decision I became acutely aware that I did not belong to Daddy Mac. His name wasn't mine—I was only borrowing it. I only pretended to be like other families. He wasn't my daddy. I didn't have a daddy.

Somewhere along my path, I learned about adoption. From that moment on I was obsessed with adoption. It was a way I could be Daddy Mac's and he could be mine. It became the third of my three secrets. I wanted a real daddy.

Shortly after the gun-to-Mama's-head incident, Mama asked me for the first and last time if we should leave Daddy Mac. Even though that night had terrified me. Even though I was mad at him for weeks. Even though a part of me hated him for that night and for the many, many other horrific nights, I looked into her eyes, with tears streaming down my face, and said, "No. No, we can't leave him. Please…"

Plain and simple, we both loved him, and I wanted a daddy.

During my entire childhood, I thought about adoption. It was always there surrounding my heart with hope. Adoption would give me a daddy. Every day, every month, year after year. Adoption was a beacon, a mecca. Adoption was the thing that would gather me in and make me part of a real family. It was also a disappointment. At birthdays. Every Christmas. Every time there was a "surprise" for me, the surprise was that it WASN'T adoption. Every year that went by and it didn't happen, disappointment swelled in my breast, choking me. Each time I felt more and more like a stepchild. Like an imposter using the name McKee.

CHAPTER 14

*"Older men declare war. But it is the youth that
must fight and die." Herbert Hoover*

Daddy Mac was a World War II vet. He suffered recurrent pain not only from a broken neck but from the horrific memories associated with liberating the world from tyranny. His specific role in rescuing and perpetuating freedom was played out as a Navy seaman off the island of Guam.

December 7, 1941 "—a date which will live in infamy..." When Franklin D. Roosevelt uttered these immortal words over the airwaves it would become one of the most famous speeches in American history heard by over 81% of the population. As Roosevelt expostulated the villainy of Japan Daddy Mac, along with the nation, listened in horror as the evil unprovoked attack perpetrated on Pearl Harbor was laid before the people.

Shortly after the Pearl Harbor assault and across the Date Line, Japan attacked Guam in a similar manner. On December 8 worshipers had gathered for the Feast Of Immaculate Conception when nine Japanese planes began bombing everything from the churches to the Pan American Hotel on Orote point in Guam.

Daddy Mac, his contemporaries and thousands of servicemen and women continued to follow the dastardly deeds of the Japanese Army on the radio. They listened in unbelief as the Japanese continued their march toward domination.

The next day, December 9, the planes continued to rain death from the sky again striking military facilities and the Pan American Airways station. And on December 10 the Japanese invaded Guam with just under 7,000 men.[iii]

In stark contrast to the invader's numbers, the military workforce stationed on Guam—mostly non-combative personnel and woefully unprepared for the surprise attack—consisted of 274 Navy, 153 Marines, and 120 Insular Force Guard. Their weapons numbered 7 machine guns, 6 pistols, and 147 rifles. The majority of their firearms were from World War I and were labeled "Do Not Shoot—For Training Only".

The invasion of Guam by the Imperial Army was paramount to shooting fish in a barrel.
The native Chamorro people resisted the despotic and murderous invaders by overt and covert means. Preferably when out of earshot and as often as possible, men, women, and children sang this ditty—if not a call to action, at least a resistance to tyranny.:

Eighth of December 1941

> *People went crazy, right here in Guam.*
> *Oh, Mr. Sam, Sam. My dear Uncle Sam,*
> *Won't you please come back to Guam.*

Caught even humming the tune would invite "binta"—a slap across the face.[iv]

The Chamorro people were used and abused in every imaginable way. Forced confinement, humiliation, beatings, rapes, torture, starvation, execution, and massacre. Neither sex nor age was exempt. Everyone was expected to bow one of the three accepted bowing forms to any Japanese encountered.

Beheadings were commonplace. Chamorro were forced to dig graves and then they were strategically placed around the holes as witnesses to their friends and relatives dropping into their final resting places.

One of the many cruel practices of the Japanese army was to dangle dogs up in trees by their hind legs to practice the art of beheading. Later they conscripted Chamorro men to hunt down and shoot every dog on the island, the rationale being that the dogs would alert islanders of Japanese patrols.[v] [vi] This oppressive practice was the straw that broke the camel's back and spoke to the heart of Daddy Mac's philosophy. He loved dogs.

In addition to the indignation, the horror, the unbelief, and the shock America felt at being plunged into war with the bombing of Pacific islands, Daddy Mac was patriotic to his very core. Always being an adventurous soul and willing, if not downright eager to plunge headlong into danger, he enlisted in the Navy.

In the **early months of 1944**, Admiral Chester W. Nimitz began his preparations for "Operation Forager". The Operation would implement the capture, occupation, and defense of the Mariana Islands which included the islands of Saipan, Tinian, and Guam.

> *"The United States Pacific forces under Nimitz's command commenced the broad Pacific sweep of island-hopping that would by mid-summer 1944 result in the Liberation of Guam."* [vii]

Daddy Mac's ship steamed in circles biding time among 274 ships and 13 aircraft carriers for fifty days in the hot summer tropical sun while the United States military strategized and began implementation of freeing Guam and her native Chamorro people from Japanese occupation…Operation Forager. [viii]

Aboard the hot and crowded battleships, carriers, cruisers, destroyers, mine vessels, patrol vessels, fleet auxiliaries, transport, and cargo vessels and landing ships & crafts, the food declined in quantity and quality; its remaining value being only the sustenance of life, culinary enjoyment being long since abandoned. Nicotine shortage began to take its toll on the nervous systems of the troops adding to the anxiety aboard the vessels of war. Daddy Mac's smoking addiction not for the last time in his life was proving to be an annoyance not worthy of maintaining the habit.[ix]

> *"The soldier is the Army. No army is better than its soldiers. The Soldier is also a citizen. In fact, the highest obligation and privilege of citizenship is that of bearing arms for one's country."*
> *George S. Patton Jr.*[x]

On **11 June 1944** Operation Forager went active, stage one. Naval and air forces began their relentless assault on Guam preparing the way for Daddy Mac and 49,999 other brave men waiting in the ships offshore. The island rocked with bombardment from 216 roaring and aggressive aircraft. [xi]

16 June 1944 Asan Beach was essential in the taking of Guam. The Japanese had fortified themselves heavily here and must be routed. Among the many steep and treacherous cliffs in Guam, there were two strategic island targets that flanked Asan Beach: Asan Point and Adelup Point known to the Chamorro as the Devils Horns.[xii] Formidable and daunting in terrain and enemy fortifications they would give the Marines charged with capturing the rugged bluffs a nearly overwhelming challenge to establish high ground inland. The Devil's Horns would live up to their name.

27 June 1944 The Navy floated off Asan Beach with four battleships, three destroyers, three cruisers, and Daddy Mac. They bombarded the Beach and the Devil's Horns and were joined by a US carrier group on 4 July and two more harbingers of death a couple of days later. [xiii]

The Chamorro huddled in caves, jungles, hollowed-out trees, and prison camps consoling themselves and their children that the bombing would bring liberation. But the unremitting deafening noise of the constant shelling highlighted the fear in their hearts that they may not survive to be free.

As the bombs continued to rain, the big gun's fire sheered trees and flattened battlements. George Tweed, a radioman first class, huddled in his cave with hope mounting in his heart for the first time since the Japanese conquest. On 10 January 1942 George and five others had escaped a forced march of prisoners being taken to board the Argentina Marie scheduled to transport the captured to a POW camp in Japan. Three of George's group were captured and beheaded; two others were captured and shot. George, the lone survivor, endured hunger, fear, great physical discomfort, loneliness, and despondency for over two and a half years in the Japanese-infiltrated jungle.

George knew his chances of surviving the bombs were slim, so he decided to try and signal one of the ships that covered the Great Pacific's horizon in Asan Bay. The Navy destroyer "The McCall" answered that miraculous distress call and rescued the grateful radioman. News of his heroic action and dramatic rescue spread among the sailors like a tonic.[xiv] Daddy Mac would tell and retell this story complete with tears streaming down his face.

10 July 1944 As Daddy Mac waited in the flotilla that fired upon Guam, the Japanese response to the bombing was to round up all civilians at gunpoint and relocate them to a central camp at Manengon. Thousands of men, women, and children were force-marched day and night through torrential downpours and blistering heat. Ankle-deep mud sucked their feet and tripped the marchers over and onto one another down the steep slopes into sharp knife-like rocks, treacherous trees, and brush that was more like buttresses stopping their rapid descent with sudden impact.

The wide column of humanity trudged through the jungle; their fearful countenances telling a shared wordless story.

> *"At a barked command, a column of soldiers with fixed bayonets began the march. The seething chaos of humans and animals compressed and uncoiled slowly, like a huge snake. Flanked by armed soldiers, the great human snake inched forward."* [xv]

During the final days of the Japanese occupation, the native Chamorro were shot on sight.

On **14 July 1944** the Navy underwater demolition teams shifted to stage two by adding their expertise to the operation and began reconnaissance. For three days the frogmen swept the beaches and cleared them of almost a thousand "obstacles" making safe conduits for Daddy Mac and the other warriors anxiously awaiting on the ships to invade. [xvi] [xvii]

W-Day. **21 July 1944. 0530** hours. Bombardment of the Devil's Horns began anew. Warships opened fire joined by airstrikes. Daddy Mac had bonded with one of his fellow sailors and as war often does it wrapped its arms around the men drawing them close physically, mentally, and psychologically. In the early morning hours as they prepared to launch the attack on Guam the two men exchanged watches as a token of friendship, agreeing to trade back when this day was over.

> *"The true soldier fights not because he hates what is in front of him, but because he loves what is behind him."* G.K. Chesterton

0819 hours. Daddy Mac loaded into the landing craft along with his friend and other brothers-in-arms. He was a 29-year-old Navy

Seaman in many ways still wet behind the ears amidst older and younger Marines, Sailors, Soldiers, and Coast Guard.

The forecast had called for clear and sunny skies with a light wind—perfect weather for freeing an enslaved people and regaining a United States Territory.[xviii] The Chamorro had depended on America for their protection for 43 years until the Japanese came.[xix] The time had come to make good on our promise of freedom to the Chamorro given by signing the Treaty of Paris in 1898.[xx] Operation Forager shifted into stage three.

Guam's heavy surf and wide reefs had been accounted for in the planning, but they were made even more treacherous by the lack of visibility. The sunny skies forecasted were obscured by thick, heavy gray and black cannon smoke caused by long days and nights of bombardment by both sides.[xxi]

The intrepid landing crafts cruised toward the island with only one objective: FREEDOM. Despite the smokey air, the Japanese saw them coming.

> *"The traces of crafts' wakes were really beautiful, Like floating threads of a loom. ... Then I realized the enemy would soon be invading the beach..."*
> 2nd Lt. Yasuhiro Yamashita, Third Battalion of the Japanese 18th Regiment

0829 hours. The first wave of landing crafts hit the beach. The island's occupiers hidden in, beneath, and behind the cliffs of the Devil's Horns began firing on the flotilla of servicemen. Thunderous rounds from the Japanese 96 25 mm AT/AA anti-aircraft guns exploded in and around the landing crafts.[xxii] They detonated in the crafts, in the water, in the men. Daddy Mac watched in horror as his friend recoiled backward from a shell's impact. Spewing blood covered his lifeless body and ran down his arm over Daddy Mac's watch as he toppled into the beautiful blue-green tropical water of the Philippine Sea becoming one of the 1,866 American servicemen who gave their lives to free the Chamorro and Guam from tyranny.[xxiii]

There was no time for grief; that would come later. The landing craft hummed on toward the Devil's Horns. The gunfire increased as they neared Asan Beach, some of the craft already disembarking their troopers.

Daddy Mac forced the image of his dying friend from his mind and joined the other men in a warrior roar that crescendoed toward the shore. As he stood to disembark machine-gun fire ripped across the landing craft. Daddy Mac fell to the beach, the sand wet beneath his body.

For three days Daddy Mac was spared some suffering as he drifted in and out of consciousness. The USS Solace steamed into the Asan harbor on 24 July 1944 her white paint gleaming mercy. Red crosses painted on her sides and her smokestacks promised relief from misery. The hospital ship was like manna from heaven. By the end of the war, the USS Solace would receive six Medals of Honor. Daddy Mac received five medals, two of which he shared with the hospital ship: The American Campaign Medal and the Asiatic-Pacific Campaign Medal-3 tours. [xxiv]

Navy doctors aboard the USS Solace treated and repaired Daddy Mac's neck broken in three places, but it was the Navy nurses he raved about for the rest of his life.

Daddy Mac often tearfully retold stories of his recuperation and rehabilitation in a Navy hospital succored by faithful Navy nurses. My young mind and heart caught hold of the heroic tales and exploits of these selfless women. I wanted to be like them. I wanted to be a nurse.

One summer in Bible school the children were asked what they wanted to be. I proudly announced I was going to be a Navy nurse and go all over the world healing people in the name of Jesus! That never came to be, but I began in earnest nursing and doctoring my animals.

CHAPTER 15

> *"Our task must be to free ourselves by widening our circle of compassion to embrace all living creatures and the whole of nature and its beauty."*
> <u>Albert Einstein</u>

I'd always loved animals and Daddy Mac did too, so he rarely said no to having pets. The apartments we lived in limited my selection…somewhat. I commandeered a grasshopper from a bush and kept it in an empty cigar box. I'm pretty sure Daddy Mac had smoked each and every cigar. The box was complete with food, (grass), water, (a beer bottle lid), and toys (a button). I was convinced the grasshopper could intelligently respond with a yes or no to questions posed to it. We had a good run, but, of course, he didn't make it through the harsh Midwest winter.

Once when visiting Grandpa and Grandma during Christmas the men went coyote hunting. Daddy Mac came home with a gunny sack full of baby coyotes, one of which we took back to our apartment. We named him Mac and raised him as a puppy, the landlord, naturally, being unaware. As Mac grew into puberty it became apparent even to me that we could not continue to keep him. He nervously paced from window to window at night and howled during the day; the landlord became very aware.

After much searching, Daddy Mac found the perfect place for Coyote Mac…the local zoo. With mixed emotions, I piled into the car for the trip to Mac's new home. We left him with the zookeeper, and I drowned my sorrow by visiting all the other animals. I hated that they had to live in cages. Daddy Mac drowned his sorrow in a bottle of schnapps.

Over the years many animals came and went, but one never quite forgets their first dog. Technically mine was a bird dog. We had him for such a short time I don't even remember his name. He literally tore up the bathroom and made so much racket the landlord put his foot down. I don't know where he went; I only know he went. But, my second dog, now he was the dog of my youth. Skeeter.

Daddy Mac was working a job out of town; Mama and I jumped on the train to go visit him. It was my first time on a train and I'm reasonably sure it was Mama's, too. "Jumped on the train" sounds so casual and it was anything but. We were awestruck and very excited. We certainly had never gone anywhere by ourselves that compared to this. Years later as an adult I visited that train station and stood in the doorway where Mama and I had walked through to get on the train. It was a scrapbook moment.

We stayed in a hotel for a few days in the small town where Daddy Mac was working. He worked during the day, and we spent most evenings at the local bar. Daddy Mac had an uncanny ability to drink all night and be a functioning human being the next day. This proficiency allowed Daddy Mac to be a good provider although he wouldn't splurge on trivials. We never lacked anything basic such as food, clothing, shelter, liquor and tobacco. So many of Daddy's friends seemed destitute…of family, home, and financial means.

I made friends with another little girl who showed up each day outside the tavern. Her parents were not part of the bar group and there didn't seem to be anyone nearby who looked after her. One day we were discussing prayer and she told me about a church where we could light candles for each prayer we said. I thought that sounded like the most wonderful thing I had ever heard.

As we made our way down the sidewalk my head swarmed with visions of candlelight prayers making their way to heaven. I began to mentally compose my prayer list.

We entered the church quietly through an enormous heavy wooden door. I came to a sudden stop. My eyes were transfixed on the beautiful stained glass windows overlooking a suffering Jesus on the Cross. My new friend took hold of my arm and pulled me toward a table full of candles. I'd never seen so many candles and I'm quite sure my mouth had been gaping open since our arrival.

Some of the candles were already lit and I wondered about the people for whom the prayers had been said. Did they know a candle was burning for them? My companion picked up a long slender taper, held it to a flame until it, too, was burning, then used it to light a candle. She then bowed her head and said a prayer before repeating the process.

I followed suit, lighting several candles, and accompanying each one with a simple prayer. I was quite sure God was listening because the trail of candle smoke ascended up and up until I could no longer see the wispy whispered prayer. My friend and I looked at one another and grinned. It sure felt good to pray.

Suddenly a harsh voice erupted from the darkened side of the room. A man dressed in midnight black appeared beside us simultaneously scolding and relieving us of our tapers. He wanted to see our dimes, which obviously neither of us had. Apparently, the price of a prayer was ten cents. We couldn't light a candle without the dime, and we couldn't say our prayers if we didn't light a candle.

I looked at the sky as he unceremoniously escorted us from the church. Regardless of what he said, at least a few of my prayers were safely on their way to Jesus.

"You think those dogs will not be in heaven! I tell you they will be there long before any of us."
Robert Louis Stevenson

It seemed like the same group of people appeared each evening in the bar. Daddy Mac worked with some of them and others just congregated around him. He was a pied piper of sorts for bar hoppers. He usually picked up the bar tab, his jokes were funny, his antics entertaining, his stories riveting and his singing and guitar playing enticed all the good-timers to our table. Our table being several pushed together in the center of the bar; we were just one big happy family. The owner didn't mind Daddy Mac taking over; afterall, the good-timers kept the drinks flowing and the cash register ringing.

There were always extra women at our table. Women were enthralled with Daddy Mac. Women who lavished attention on him whether Mama was there or not. Women who were the cause of Mama's secret heartache. When the bar closed each evening, we walked to our apartment where Daddy Mac would ironically accuse Mama of flirting, slap her around for a while then pass out until waking up unusually cheerful and chipper; ready for another day of work, wine, women, and merrymaking.

One lady, Jackie, who frequented our table had a dog. A tiny black dog with kindred spirit eyes. I stared at him captured by his innocence lit with a spark of inherent chutzpa. Skeeter. I was in love. Skeeter and I became fast friends; neither of us enjoyed the evening's festivities at the ash-laden beer-soaked table. I held him, I walked him, I talked to him. At some point, Jackie, having gotten under the influence very early that day, in a grand gesture gave Skeeter to me. The other patrons cheered and applauded; Jackie basked in well-doing. Daddy Mac was effulgent. Skeeter and I were ecstatic.

Skeeter had a little red harness and a red leash. I walked him up and down the block. Sometimes we were in the streetlights, sometimes it was dark. But I wasn't afraid. I had Skeeter. We discussed the foolishness of adults and planned wonderful woody outings for when we got home.

On the last night of our little vacation, once again the group was assembled around several bar tables crammed together. Drinks had been flowing, cheers made, and drunken good-byes in the offing. I sat at the improvised table with Skeeter on my lap. Jackie said it was time to go, stood up, and took hold of Skeeter. Daddy Mac jumped up and grabbed Skeeter mid-air. Glasses and bottles tipped over as the uneven table jostled. Daddy and Jackie were exchanging words, Skeeter's eyes were bulging, and I was still holding onto his leash not quite sure of what was happening.

Daddy Mac being a formidable opponent, bolstered by the keg of beer and the sips of whiskey from the flask he secretly carried in his pocket and armed with righteous indignation at the audacity of anyone trying to take a child's pet away from her, let alone *his* child's pet, won the tug-of-dog-war handily. Skeeter was truly mine.

Skeeter was my companion well into my teens. He tolerated the doll clothes and the beauty salon shampoos; he loved exploring the woods, chasing chickens, enduring the pet raccoon, and sleeping in my bed. He comforted me during the dark times and helped me celebrate the good. He listened to my secrets, barked at my enemies, but fell short of homework answers. When I fell in love with my future husband, Skeeter tolerated him.

Anyone who had an animal misfit knew where to bring them. Once a neighbor showed up with a tiny black piglet with a swarth of white around its middle. Mama Pig had accidentally stepped on him splaying his side wide and deep.

Daddy Mac picked up the pig and looked at me. "Don't just stand there, give me a hand," he said. Mama brought out some cloths, hydrogen peroxide, and a threaded needle. I poured the peroxide into the wound, and it immediately foamed over. I hurriedly and clumsily wiped away the bubbles and Daddy Mac took the first stitch. You've never heard a pig squeal until it's been stuck with a needle. Over and over.

We finished the job and I burst with pride. I was a nurse! The pig turned out to be a girl and I named her Tippy—her tail looked like it had been dipped in white paint Tippy and Skeeter became friends and Tippy thought she was more dog than pig. She followed us around the farm all day, but Mama insisted she sleep in the barn at night.

On laundry day, Mama would roll out the wringer washer and the double rinse bins. Then she'd sort the whites and darks into piles on the floor. She left the back door open to go back and forth to the clothesline. Tippy loved laundry day. She trotted confidently into the house and rooted under a pile of sorted clothes to take a piggy nap. Mama was startled more than once while picking up dirty clothes and swore one of these days she would accidentally throw Tippy into the washer. Tippy loved rooting over Skeeter's food and water dishes leaving the mess behind as she walked her piggy-self all over the house finding mischief in every corner.

One day I came home from school, got Skeeter from the house, and took off for the barn. The barnyard was strangely quiet. Tippy's oinks and grunts did not greet me. I looked in the barn, behind the water trough, under the swing, in the chicken house. No Tippy. I called her, I shouted for her and inevitably I pleaded for her. Finally, I ran back to the house thinking perhaps Mama had relinquished and let Tippy inside.

Mama sat at The Table. I noticed Daddy Mac wasn't home. But more importantly, where was Tippy? I didn't even have to ask her the question. Mama looked at me through unfallen tears. My worst nightmare had come to pass. In days past I had blocked out all talk of the neighborhood butcher. That plan was for other pigs. That plan was for ordinary pigs. That plan was for cruel, heartless, and mean people who ate their pigs. It was years before I ever ate bacon again and days before I spoke to Daddy Mac.

There's something about a lamb that melts all negative notions about animals. It was late one night. The moon was full lighting up the yard with its silver mystery. Daddy Mac and a friend had been off on some excursion, probably replenishing the liquor supply.

Mama and I were sitting outside at the picnic table trying to stay cool and swatting mosquitoes. Daddy Mac's car pulled up into our drive then he came walking across the lawn with something cradled in his arms. When he came closer, I saw the little black face and big black eyes of a small sheep staring at me. Suddenly it began to bleat, over and over and over. I was all smiles and insisted on holding her. She wasn't a tiny newborn. She was old enough to be weaned and too big for me to hold. She was kicking and crying and not at all as happy to see me as I was to see her.

Daddy Mac carried her to the barn, and we bedded her down for the night. Now, just where does one obtain a lamb in the middle of the night? I had a suspicion that some farmer was short a lamb come morning, but I never got the real story and at that time in my life I really didn't care.

Skeeter and I spent the whole next day with the lamb. She eventually calmed down and even began to like me. She never thought much of Skeeter. Heaven only knows why I named her Jackie given the trauma Skeeter and I went through with that name. But Jackie it was.

Her wool fascinated me. Having never been anywhere near sheep the only wool I knew anything about was Daddy Mac's Pendleton shirts. In fact, I was quite surprised to learn that Pendleton was wool and originally came from a sheep. One of the wonders of my small world.

Jackie thrived. Daddy Mac got me another female and an outstanding show-quality male. I'm pretty sure he paid for these. The next year Jackie was expecting, and I just couldn't believe we were going to have a baby lamb. I pampered her and we talked about when she would be a mother.

I explained to Skeeter that he probably would not be allowed in Jackie's stall after the baby came. Not only were no boys allowed, but dogs were also banned. I'm sure Mama grew tired of the conversation always coming round to Jackie and her baby.

The months dragged on until finally, it was time. Daddy Mac said it would be any day now. The snow was gone; the Ozark hills were courting Spring. During morning chores I knew something wasn't quite right with Jackie. The future Navy nurse in me sensed Jackie was in distress even though my young mind didn't have a clue what was wrong.

I ran to the bedroom and frantically begged a groggy Daddy Mac to come have a look. He shooed me out to meet the school bus promising he would check in on Jackie.

I usually loved being at school, but this day my eyes would not stop searching out the old clock hanging above the chalk board ticking out its agonizing seconds.

The school bus had no more than rolled to a stop in front of my house when I jumped off and ran to the barn. No Jackie. Mama met me in the barnyard and said Daddy Mac and a friend had taken Jackie to the vet.

In just a short time our old black Lincoln drove up and I could see Daddy Mac behind the wheel. As I ran toward the car I noticed the back seat had been removed and was laying under the tree beside the driveway. It was a common occurrence to remove the backseat for transporting animals, feed, or lawnmowers. It came in handy for farm projects when the old truck wouldn't start. I looked through the car window and there was Daddy Mac's friend in the back with Jackie laying across his lap.

I thought she was resting as she didn't raise her head when I called her name. Daddy Mac's friend was very tender-hearted especially with a few beers under his belt and he began to cry. That old familiar feeling of dread and fear engulfed me. I'd been down this road before.

It would be a few years before I understood exactly what Jackie had died from…toxemia. Eclampsia in humans. I tormented myself on what I probably did wrong to cause her death. Daddy Mac and his friend carried Jackie out to the back pasture. The frozen ground combined with the rocky terrain prevented her burial, so I spent some time in vain trying to cover her with rocks.

The next morning, I went out to pay my youthful respects and the sight struck horror into my heart. The coyotes had ripped her apart. Her beautiful wool was blood-soaked and ragged. A shocking gaping hole in her middle led my eyes to the two little mangled bundles lying beside her. Twins. She was having twins. My grief was magnified. My heart was broken.

It seemed that life was taking me through dark tunnels. I didn't understand it then but now I see it helped me to not only reach for the strength within but to reach toward God. The nurturing that was lacking in my home was waiting in abundance in my Heavenly Father and His Son. I didn't think of God as my Father then, but I did turn to Jesus Christ. The summers spent in Bible school opened the door to His Glorious Presence. I found myself relying on Him in my trusting childlike ways. I trusted He would always be there, and He always was.

So many times, year after year, and in so many ways in times of distress, abandonment, and misery I felt unrealistically comforted. I didn't realize it then, but the Holy Spirit poured out upon me. I was safe. And I would be ok. No matter the depth of desolation and wretchedness I happened to be in at the time, Happiness always found me. My Pollyanna persona that some people make fun of was God's gift to me. It was a vehicle for me to follow Goodness into the Light. That hope perched in my heart that I mentioned? A huge part of it was centered on Christ. That hope always came through. I'm thankful for the Love Jesus offered me. And I'm thankful I accepted it.

> *"Now, God be praised, that to believing souls*
> *gives light in darkness, comfort in despair."*
> *William Shakespeare*

Daddy Mac's uncle, Grandma Lizzy's brother, was a force to be reckoned with. Uncle Willie was kind and fun and somewhat of a rebel. It's no wonder he and Daddy Mac were best buds. His laughter was always ready to burst out of him like a happiness balloon. Once when Daddy Mac and I were on a 'coon hunting expedition we discovered a comfortable den in a tree filled with warm, wiggly, fuzzy little masked bodies. Baby raccoons make this wonderful little whirring sound. I call it their Me Song. I imagined them singing for the sheer joy of living. Joy of being themselves, of just *BEING*.

Of course, one of those babies ended up in my arms, in my bed, in my heart. And, of course, I had to name him Willie because he had that funny indomitable spirit of Uncle Willie.

Willie is the first of a long line of animals I fed with a tiny doll bottle filled with milk. I nurtured him religiously by feeding him every few hours night and day. Willie was a cat with thumbs. There was no door he could not open, no curtain he could not climb and no heart he could not melt. My little masked bandit played tag with Skeeter, stole crackers off the cabinet, wrestled with—yes—our 'coon dog, "Blue". Blue was the pride of the county and had proven himself time and again with his 'coon hunting prowess. Yet he and Willy were the best of friends and the enigma of the neighborhood. Some mysteries are never solved.

Willie grew into puberty and beyond. He took his newfound manliness on the road disappearing overnight at first then for two or three days at a time. We had a well just outside the kitchen covered by its own cute short little house. Willie was fingering the shingles on the wellhouse, and I casually put my arm around him as I had done a thousand times. He responded with a snarl. I suppose that was his warning, which I completely ignored. In a flash he bit my thumb, penetrating completely through the nail. The pain I felt was beyond the physical; it was a betrayal.

Mama nursed, comforted, and consoled me. Daddy Mac said to toughen up. Willie was just being a raccoon. It seemed harsh at the time, but Daddy Mac taught me the world is hard and if we want to "get along" in it we need to buck up and be a soldier. We need to take it on the chin and not whine. Inside I was a girly girl, soft-hearted, shy and sensitive. But I wanted to be Daddy's girl. Plain and simple, I wanted his approval so when we moved to the country, I transformed into the tomboy son. I didn't realize what I was doing at the time, but the desire to win his love, to have a real daddy, and be adopted drove my decisions and molded my character.

I ignored the throbbing pain in my hand, took Skeeter, and went out to feed the chickens.

Willie rarely came home after that. Periodically we'd see him in the yard at night raiding Blue's food. A friend who lived down on the lake said he had a raccoon couple who stayed at the edge of the water in some trees. It appeared to be a big male with a smaller female. Later in the spring they had little ones and made quite a spectacle for our friends' visitors. He thought it was Willie. Of course, there was no telling for certain, but it sure made me feel good thinking about Willie with a family.

DADDY TRAILS

"If having a soul means being able to feel love and loyalty and gratitude, then animals are better off than a lot of humans".
James Herriot, <u>All Creatures Great and Small</u>

There was something about nature, fresh air, trees, and wild animals that beckoned me. Part of it was freedom from the cramped smokey apartments I had always known. But it went deeper than just an escape *from* something. It was a calling *to* something. I loved, loved, loved being outside. Regardless of winter or summer the wild child within explored, hunted, climbed trees, and forded creeks with faithful companion Skeeter.

I hiked a mile to harvest watercress out of a lovely, cold, clear spring. I built tree houses because you can never have too many places to retreat. I commandeered the brooder house to set up tiny tables with tea sets. I spent hours in the swing dreaming up future projects, planning ways to hoist even larger boards up into even higher branches of the current treehouse endeavor. I had no siblings which circled back to my first secret—I wanted a baby in the house. I wanted a brother or sister and since it was too late for a BIG brother, I wanted a sister with all my being. I had friends at school, and at home I had my animals. I was in my element, but I still prayed for siblings.

To most people Rocky and Bullwinkle were cartoons. Except for my granddaughter and I. Today she has two chickens with these familiar monikers, and as a child, I had two squirrels. Again, they were rescued babies hand-fed with a doll bottle. I went through a lot of doll bottles. They were beautiful fox squirrels and very lively. They didn't get to stay in the house as long as Willie had; they were just too squirrely.

Daddy Mac built them a huge cage outside. I became their keeper and faithfully cleaned the cage and gave them fresh water, elm buds, and nuts. By mid-summer, it was apparent even to me that they would prefer to be free. One day I took a breath, opened the cage door, stepped back, and waited. It took them a while to work up the courage to come out. They jumped to the ground, sniffed around, jumped back up onto the cage, thought for a minute, then flew off the cage, into the grass, and down the hill at a dead run.

They stopped only once to look back as if to say goodbye. It's impossible to tell if they were among the scores of squirrels I would see in the yard and on excursions into the woods. Daddy Mac was proud of me for letting them go and I savored his praise—a few and far-between moment.

CHAPTER 16

"You may be as different as the sun and the moon, but the same blood flows through both your hearts. You need her, and she needs you..."
George R.R. Martin

The three of us, Daddy Mac, Mama, and I were sitting on bar stools at Harry's Place our local pub. It was early afternoon; Daddy Mac was drinking a beer and Mama was uncharacteristically drinking a glass of water. I probably had a coke, my drink of preference at 12 years of age.

I didn't notice it at first until the conversation turned to *why* she was drinking water. Daddy Mac said the word pregnant which embarrassed Mama to a bright pink.

Pregnant? Pregnant!! Mama was going to have a baby!!! A baby! For me!! From that moment on I claimed it as my own. I thought about it. I dreamed about it. My first secret wish was coming true!!! Daddy Mac continued his lifestyle as though everything was the same. But, to me, *nothing* was the same and it never would be again.

Mama and I planned, and talked, and planned. Someone arranged a baby shower at our house, and it was the most exciting thing. I was used to lots of people visiting, but it always involved bawdy behavior, booze, and belligerence. This time it would be all women. Sober women.

This time instead of liquor there would be cake. Instead of lewd, crude, and rude jokes, there would be talk of babies and bonnets and blankets.

For weeks I remained in a state of euphoria. I sailed through my days thinking of the shower and drifted off to sleep whispering shower details to Skeeter. My first and last prayer of the day was in thankfulness for my baby. For this was, without a doubt, my baby. I planned on taking care of it and loving it forever. I didn't care if it was a boy or girl, I would after years of dreaming have a sibling. But down deep, a sister would be heavenly.

Mama said it should arrive around my birthday. That sealed it for me. It would be my special birthday present from God. It really would be mine!

I don't think Mama drank during her pregnancy, but she did continue to smoke. In those days no one thought a thing about it.

It was right after lunch. I was at Edmonson school—my one-room schoolhouse perched in the middle of the country that I had totally loved since day one. It had been three years since leaving the city and it had flown by. I considered everyone at Edmonson my friend and best of all, I was theirs.

On this day, I had put away my lunch box and returned to my desk. The room was decked out with handmade Christmas ornaments of which I was very proud. The cold gravel in the drive crunched as a car drove in. We almost never had any visitors during school hours, so all eyes were on the window.

The teacher rose and went to the door; their voices were low so all we could hear were faint murmurs as she conversed with someone. She turned and came directly towards me. I had no warning of impending doom.

It turned out to be Harry of Harry's Place, the owner/operator of the country bar and a good family friend. The teacher said I was to go with him to the hospital. No other information was given to me but the look and feel of sadness permeated even my child's mind and heart. I started to panic as I put on my coat. Something had happened to Mama. I just knew it.

We drove in silence time stretching beyond its measure making the ride interminable. When we eventually reached the hospital, my insides felt as cold and barren as the icicles hanging from the naked tree branches. We walked in the door and Daddy Mac was waiting; grief had smothered the convivial good-timer. He looked broken. I burst into tears as he embraced me just knowing my Mama was dead.

When he said our baby had been born, I looked at him in shock. I had never even considered that; it wasn't time. Mama was ok. Baby was here. Joy began to gurgle up through my system. Baby was here!!! And it was a girl!! I had a sister. It took me a few minutes to realize no one else was happy. Sadness still hung in the room like the low-hanging winter storm clouds outside the hospital.

I knew it was still two months before our baby was supposed to be born, but I didn't realize the implications of the timeline. The doctor had told Daddy Mac our baby girl was very sick and probably wouldn't live. My world crashed. Mama was ok, but our baby wasn't. My sister wasn't.

She hung on for two days. For two days I wasn't alone. For two days I had a sister, Baby Wanda Lynn. Tears of anguish dissolved my plans for her and I and Skeeter. I have no idea when they told me she had died; I think it is just too painful to remember. I lived the next few days in a sorrowful fog. I don't remember Mama coming home from the hospital. Or, Grandma Lizzy and Grandpa and aunts, uncles and my cousins coming for the funeral. I don't remember if Daddy Mac left the whiskey in the bottle or consumed it to dull his own pain.

I only remember the funeral. The tiny, tiny baby lying in the tiny, tiny casket. Her sweet little face looked like a sleeping doll. I couldn't take my eyes off her as I sat on the front pew with Daddy Mac and Mama. This was the second time I had been in this beautiful little church.

For months I had been deliriously happy but now I had fallen into the abyss. My first secret wish lay crushed and broken. My sister had been given and taken faster than a spring lightning strike. I sat dry-eyed and silent in the pew staring at my sister. If tears are limited in number, then I had already used all of mine. I wondered how much time I had; when would they close her up? Panic welled within me. I would never see her again. I had to keep my eyes on her; memorize every tiny perfect feature. I tried not to blink.

Then, the preacher stopped talking. Some men stood up and went toward the casket. I wanted to scream, to stop them from shutting that lid. To stop them from taking away my baby.

I only remember one thing from the days, the weeks or even the months following the death of my sister. Daddy Mac had several episodes of what is known in the tavern-world of "crying the blues". Liquor consumed any rational thought, and he would rant about the funeral sermon. According to Daddy Mac the preacher said little Wanda Lynn was going to hell because of the life Daddy Mac and Mama lived. For years, Grandma Lizzy always claimed that the preacher never said any such thing. That it was just Daddy Mac's conscience.

I didn't know either way. I only knew that the God I loved would never ever send my baby to live in hell. If anyone lived in hell, it was me.

CHAPTER 17

*"They seemed to suddenly come upon happiness
as if they had surprised a butterfly in a winter wood."*
Edith Wharton

I loved Edmonson school. In the big city school, I was shy and often pretended not to know the answers to questions. The teacher at Edmonson treated me with kindness and patience and it seemed like she really cared about me. One day she took me onto her lap, I don't remember the reason or her response. I only remember how I felt. Accepted. Acknowledged. Loved. From that day forward I cared about my grades, took an interest in school, and adored my classmates. I loved each school morning and hated the weekends. My mind opened to learning; my soul blossomed.

Edmonson introduced me to many new things, one of which was the lunch box. I carried my food and later my treasures in a variety of tin boxes made just for the purpose of taking food to school. I marveled at such a thing and chose my lunchbox with great care and unbridled enthusiasm of a neophyte. The lunch box was a small square tin with a handle and came in a variety of colors and styles suitable either for the timid or the more adventurous, audacious soul. It included a small thermos bottle that fit snuggly inside and matched the design on the outside of the lunchbox. In the three and a half years I attended

Edmonson I had two of those paragons of food transportation. The first one was a tartan plaid. I knew nothing of Scots, Scotland, or their mode of dress except that Mama always said we were Scotch, Irish and English. I would one day learn that Scottish blood comprises thirty percent of my heritage.

The second and last lunch box, and my all-time favorite, had a picture of Hop-a-long Cassidy and his beautiful white horse named Topper. I was right in the middle of my "Hop-A-Long boots and a pistol that shoots" phase. I adored Hop-A-Long's white horse and I'm quite sure it influenced my desire and love for white clothing. Unfortunately, Daddy Mac didn't share that ideal. He never let me have white anything except socks and underwear. Looking back I can see it probably had to do with the penchant for white clothing to get dirty very quickly, especially on a rootin-tootin, tree-climbing, cap-gun-toting grade-schooler. Since laundry was only done once a week, I'm sure it saved my Mama a boatload of work.

I loved cowboys. I crooned along with Gene Autry and Roy Rogers. I especially loved Trigger, Roy Rogers horse. I pretended to be like Roy's side-kick and wife Dale Evans and practiced drawing and firing my six-shooter cap gun at the unsuspecting and unaffected chickens. Skeeter played the part of Rin-Tin-Tin.

I saw a picture of Trigger receiving his own kilt while he was in Scotland. Seeing Trigger's picture with the plaid draped over his hindquarters stirred the Scottish blood within me and served to enhance the enchantment with my first plaid lunch box.

I marveled at the tricks Trigger could perform and later learned that Trigger had over 150 tricks in his repertoire. He could sign his name with a pencil, never mind that it was just an X. When he took a nap, he covered himself with a blanket. The best trick was when he walked on his hind legs, I loved that. And, although Skeeter resisted most of the tricks I tried to teach him, we somewhat succeeded with the two hind-leg walk.

Mama scoffed at all Trigger's tricks we watched on our small black and white television but she thought the one we couldn't see was his best all-time accomplishment. Trigger was housebroken.

My years at Edmonson delineated my transformation from city girl to country girl. I traded dresses for jeans. Lunchrooms for lunch boxes. Walking to school for tiny school buses. Bullies for friends. Hopscotch for softball. Hating school for loving school.

Even today when I make my annual pilgrimage on Memorial Day to my girlhood haunts I go by Edmonson. I squint to see through the overgrown brush to see its little white frame. It has undergone many transformations over the years from school to derelict, to homestead, and back to vacant. Now, the tiny white clapboard building is gone completely. But I will always see it in my heart: the door standing ajar, children contending the appointed umpires call in the makeshift ball diamond over being safe at first, or teamwork in hauling water to Outhouse Hill to make an ice slide in the dead of winter. I remember the blinding pain on the pitcher's mound when a softball hit me between the eyes. I remember hula-hoop contests, spelling bees, best buddies, and first boyfriends. I can still smell the smoke from the old wood stove in the center of the room, hear the floor creak as you approach the blackboard, feel the warm embrace of my teacher, and witness a shy sickly little girl slowly become a young woman.

CHAPTER 18

"Friendship improves happiness and abates misery, by, the doubling of our joy, and dividing of our grief;" - Joseph Addison

There was a new girl in school. I had met her before everyone else at Edmonson, at Harry's Place. Harry and Minnie's establishment had a bar in front and living quarters in the back. On one side it sported a short bar lined with stools and a jukebox at the end of the room. I loved that jukebox. On the other end of the room were the check-out counter, a deep freezer, and a small empty space that served as a dance floor. I spent many a night listening to music, dancing the two-step or a waltz with Daddy Mac, or just clapping and tapping.

The community was abuzz with the new folks in town. Penny and I were instant friends. We were one year apart in age. We were both only children. We both had a stepdad. Our parents shared the love of drinking the night away. Best of all, she would also go to school at Edmonson and allow us further time to bond over our shared circumstances at home.

I spent nights at her house and she at mine. She had her faithful dog Sparks, I had Skeeter. Her home was literally a small one-room tar-paper shack with no heat and no water. There was a makeshift counter where her mother prepared their food and two beds—a double for her parents and a single for Penny—side by side. At least, I told her, she had a real bed.

The Osage River meandered slowly toward the sea between large imposing bluffs close to Penny's property. The popular Kaysinger Bluff lay up the river a few miles a favorite peeve of Daddy Mac's; he hated tourists. The hills and bluffs were a large part of Penny's and my explorations. We found a small cave in the bluffs and proceeded to furnish it with our girl stuff. We cleaned out nature's debris, rolled stones into appropriate places for chairs, and called it good. A home away from home.

Much to our disappointment, we never spotted the ghost of a woman with a knife through her head riding a horse who had been seen by many Missourians. We were sure she must patronize this wooded secluded area. Taverns frequented by travelers and hunters, fisherman and farmers spun yarns of ghost sightings and near-death experiences at the hands of the departed, but the elusive horse-riding she-ghost evaded Penny and I.

We thought surely we would see some spirit in these dense and deserted forests. We looked for the ghost of a stray Confederate or Union soldier killed in battle. Missouri had been an aberration during the civil war. The majority of her citizens were confederate but refused to succeed from the Union. Missouri eventually, at least politically, took up the Union's cause creating a hotbed of incivility.

Since the mighty river was named for their tribe—the Osage—and they had camped on both sides of the river leaving behind artifacts that we collected for years, we were disappointed beyond description when we didn't even see the specter of one warrior or fair Native American maiden.

I had a knife, so Penny and I proceeded to cut and trim a few skinny tree branches with the lofty goal of toasting marshmallows, roasting wieners, and for after-dinner recreation an occasional sword fight. They also made awesome writing-in-the-dirt apparatuses and effective flags when we tied her stepdad's underwear on one end.

We made a small circle of stones for a campfire in the center of the cave, gathered kindling, and lit the fire with our contraband matches. Small spiders and bugs made a run for it as the fire gained volume. Since all four of our parents smoked, there were matches and lighters aplenty for the taking.

Instead of spiraling toward the doorway like any self-respecting smoke, the campfire smoke rose to the cave's ceiling and then proceeded to fill the entire room. With stinging eyes and burning throats we fanned the smoke toward the cave opening with our coats. We never mastered the art of fire building—we blamed it on the inevitable rain and wet kindling.

We left our own petroglyphs on the cave's interior; perhaps they would inspire future explorers. The river bluff cave proved to be our go-to refuge whenever we needed time away from the alcoholic adults in our lives. We were Sacajawea and Pocahontas—in total disregard of historical discrepancies.

Penny's step dad raised a few pigs. The colossal male who was twice the size of Penny and I put together ruled the rocky pen. His territorial high-pitched squeals could be heard far beyond his electric fence boundary. Missouri Ozark boulders are not benign, smooth, and river-worn round. They are vicious rocks with long sharp serrated edges. It's as if the ground is opening its wide treacherous jaws filled with rows of spikey teeth just waiting for unsuspecting little girls.

The mammoth pigs' teeth had grown into tusks more like a wild boar than a domestic farmyard animal. We had been instructed to stay away from the pigs, the pigpen, and especially the boar.

Funny thing about being left to your own devices so much of the time. You're so used to making your own decisions you begin to think you know everything. The outcomes that are viewed as poor choices by parents are hailed as courageous and daring adventures to intrepid girls. At ten and eleven years of age, Penny and I were convinced of our ability to outsmart, outmaneuver, and outfox any problem or situation that came our way.

Thus, when you combine tall trees and native grapevines there's only one logical conclusion. You swing from one tree to another via grapevines never mind that between the two trees lay the forbidden pigpen.

The pigs were out of sight and out of the sun in their crude shelter. There would be no better time than now.

The first attempt at crossing the great divide resulted in the grapevine breaking. Fortunately, the vine lost its hold on the overhead branch at the first jump off the limb rather than halfway into the pig pen. I tumbled down through the branches catching hold of one before I hit the ground.

Not to worry. Penny knew where her stepdad kept a rope thus keeping the escapade alive. We found the rope and weighed the ins and outs of it being able to carry us safely from one tree limb to another over the lion's lair. No matter that Tarzan used grape vines; Roy Rogers used a rope.

We climbed back up the tree dragging the rope with us. It took a while to securely tie it to a high branch. All this preparation and redesign of the plan had taken quite a bit of time. The sun was getting low on the horizon. Not only could we hear our parents beginning to mill around talking as if we were getting ready to go home, but the Great Swine of the Ozarks had also come out of his shelter into the pig yard. We had to hurry. There wasn't time to take turns, we would have to go together. We both grabbed hold of the rope, grinned at one another for support, and shoved off in tandem.

The rope creaked, and the branch bent and shook, as we arced over the pen. When we passed over him, the Great Swine looked up, opened his enormous foul mouth, and looked all the world like a hippopotamus I had seen in one of the National Geographic magazines stacked in the corner of our living room. Penny and I screamed, the boar squealed a furious shriek and Daddy Mac came running and swearing.

We hit the target tree with gale force, were simultaneously knocked loose of the rope, and clung to the closest branch wide-eyed and breathless. Our parents had reached the scene of the crime; Daddy Mac was laughing, Mama was ashen, and Penny's parents were speechless. The disappointed boar turned and sauntered toward his sows.

Penny's parents could have been the social bookend to mine. A violent atmosphere pervaded her home that mirrored my own. One rainy evening Penny and I sat in the back seat of their car headed for town in a deluge of a storm. We were to meet Mama and Daddy Mac at a popular tavern. Her parents were arguing; Penny and I were masterful at tuning out our surroundings.

The car abruptly came to a stop and her mother opened her door. Wind drove the rain inside the car and into the back seat. Penny and I huddled together under a thin blanket for protection as much from the angry shouting as from the cold wet rain. Her mother jumped out and ran to the front of the car. Penny's dad had already exited his side and ran to catch her. The car had died but the headlights were still on outlining the driving rain as it pelted them; the windshield wipers doggedly slapped back and forth. He grabbed her by the arm and slammed her down on the car, her back pressed against the hood. He was raging. The storm was raging. Penny and I remained huddled together as the wind carried all the anger and anguish across the prairie.

By the time we all walked into the bar, we were just a few more soaked patrons coming in out of the rain for refreshment and entertainment. We greeted Daddy Mac and Mama as if the prior events were the most normal thing in the world. I guess in my life they were.

"As with the butterfly, adversity is necessary to build character in people."   Joseph B. Wirthlin

It was Saturday. I used to hate Saturdays and Sundays before Penny came. They meant there was no school and thus no friends until Monday. But with Penny's arrival that all changed.

We had the entire day to ourselves at my house as our parents had gone into town. We knew they would be gone all day and possibly well into the night. We had treasures to find, trees to climb, adventures to begin. It was a magical day alternating between playing house and looking for arrowheads. We lived close to where Cole Camp Creek merged with the Osage River; natives and tourists alike found Native American artifacts most likely from the Osage tribe.

We played hard all morning and by mid-afternoon we were hungry. We searched the kitchen cupboards but for some reason, the usual peanut butter and jelly sandwich was not appealing. I stepped onto the back porch where the refrigerator and upright freezer were kept and after rummaging around I finally settled on a nice ham wrapped in butcher paper. I relished being the hostess and made a great show of unwrapping the ham and slicing it with a large butcher knife. Daddy Mac prided himself on his sharp knives, so cutting the slices was child's play.

We sat at The Table and ate until we could eat no more. We were regaling ourselves with the day's exploits giggling at every juncture when the gravel in the driveway signaled its usual message. Skeeter began barking as we heard our parents getting out of the car. They were home sooner than expected, but no matter. We just hoped that Penny would not have to leave as we had great plans for the evening.

Daddy Mac was the first one to enter the house. He stood in the arch between the living room and kitchen and gawked at The Table. The ham sat in the center; its wrapping paper crumpled to one side. Awkwardly sliced pieces of ham lay on the breadboard in various shapes and sizes, and the knife smeared with ham grease lay on top. Slices of bread spilled haphazardly out of the open package. A case knife stabbed pertinently into the mayonnaise; its lid tossed aside. It was a mess to be sure but what can one expect from young girls hungry and heady with freedom.

Penny's parents had joined Daddy Mac and were staring open-mouthed at the sight. Daddy Mac, having gotten the full measure of the situation, was not happy. His question as to what did we think we were doing was answered with perfect innocence. "Eating," we replied.

Daddy Mac and the parents had been drinking all day, so I lay it to muddled thinking when he took our reply to be insolence if not outright smart-alecky sarcasm. His reprimand beginning with who gave us permission to eat the ham morphed into well, I hope you're happy because you're both going to die. He then launched into the sad and painful death we were going to experience explaining it with animated gestures sparing no gruesome detail.

Penny and I burst into tears; Mama glanced at Penny's mom with an expression I would not understand until years later. The ham had been fully cooked thus preventing any health hazard much less the possibility of death. I never asked Daddy Mac why he chose to scare us, and I never fully understood why he elected to punish us in this way. Ham is still not a favorite with me.

Penny and I were the best of pals; a similar home life welding us with bonds we weren't old enough to recognize. We laughed and played our days away. We never really overcame the sad and abusive households in which we lived, but we eventually learned to cope.

CHAPTER 19

"Neither one of us was old enough to drive a car
Sometimes it was raining, sometimes it would shine
We wore out that gravel road
between your house and mine."
Diamond Rio   <u>Meet In The Middle</u>

Country kids are better drivers. We are given sink or swim responsibility at a younger age and learn from those experiences. Driving tractors and trucks in the hay fields, rounding up strays, back and forth to the barns, to neighboring farms, to the local grocery, to the gas station, to the ol' swimmin' hole all give us years of proficiency far ahead of our city counterparts.

My first driving experience was on Grandpa's delightful Ford tractor. Oh, my cousins and I loved that tractor. When cranked up it politely belched a little puff of smoke before it settled into a gentle chug-chug rhythm. Its faded dove gray paint was worn thin in places from years of service and trimmed with lines of thin rust attesting to its many hours in the field under the blistering sun or plowing a virgin path through mountains of snow around the barn lot and out into the field making a way for the cows and pigs to forage.

The cousins and I had a few harrowing experiences learning to coordinate and navigate the intricacies of shifting gears, clutch, and brake. Once going full blast across the barnyard barreling toward the smokehouse with several of us on board, not knowing just who was in charge of the operating system, we learned team effort, trust, and how many feet in advance of the goal it took to press the brake pedal down far enough to bring the old Ford to a complete stop. The veneer of hooting laughter thinly covered the fear lurking in our inexperienced and youthful pluck. It ended well with all of us safe and high on the blissful unawareness of danger. After the initial adrenalin dissipated and our innate moxie reassembled, we were ready for the next adventure. Who can run faster than the bull?

Like every farmer who ever farmed in those days, Daddy Mac had an old pickup. I loved that truck and was allowed to drive on our country roads far in advance of the 15 years the state deemed appropriate for first-time drivers. Of course, I wasn't exactly inexperienced having had my share of turns driving Grandpa's tractor. The chipped green paint pocked with dents varying in degree of severity and the general disrepair of the truck forbore any trepidation Daddy Mac may have had as to the damage I could do it.

Therefore, I was allowed to drive the bumpy, pitted, gravel road to Edmonson. Edmonson village as opposed to Edmonson school was a small community comprised of a few small businesses and several houses nestled in one of our Ozark valleys about five miles from my house. The ill-kept rocky road to Edmonson meandered up the side of hills, down gullies, and across at least one creek. Mama always said they must have followed a black snake trail when planning the road.

Edmonson's diminutive size did not diminish its importance to the surrounding homesteads. The store supplied foodstuffs not raised on the farm and all those things one runs out of before the next scheduled trip "to town" for groceries and supplies. The little community also supplied gasoline and diesel to keep farm equipment plowing, harvesting, thrashing, and all the back-breaking tasks of running a farmstead, kerosene for emergency lamps, bait for fishermen who didn't have time or were too lazy to dig their own worms or were too fainthearted to attempt the production of stink bait and Cokes to quench the consequences of the dusty road and hot humid Missouri summers. The occasional tourist was welcomed with country charisma as they brought "outside" dollars to the fledgling businesses struggling to scratch out a living in the remote countryside.

Edmonson may have lacked the charm of an English hamlet, but it pulsed with the warmth and comradery of a country neighborhood. Farmers and farmers' wives, fishermen and hunters, children and dogs meandered around tending to their tasks gathering Wonder bread, fish hooks, or gas for the tractor.

I don't remember for sure, but I imagine Edmonson did not carry such items as tobacco and alcohol. Daddy Mac either stopped at the local tavern on the way to Edmonson or traveled an additional twelve miles to one of the two rural towns large enough for at least one drinking establishment.

The Edmonson proprietors who frowned on smoking and drinking ran a Bible school in the Edmonson school building during summers when our regular school was closed. I hated the months there was no school and jumped at the chance to attend Bible School. It was here that I first encountered Jesus as someone who would, could, and did love me unconditionally, who was with me through thick and thin, who always forgave my folly and foolishness. In later years the proprietors started a modest country church.

Edmonson school that had nestled into my heart, that I couldn't wait to attend each morning, that I was loath to leave each afternoon sat just outside and over the hill from the hub of Edmonson, the tiny country commercial enterprise of groceries and gas.

Nothing diminished the sheer pleasure I felt when I was all alone driving our old truck, bumping along on the gravel road. Exhilaration fueled my mood; I loved being out by myself; out on the road, giddy with freedom, jam-packed with confidence, and headed for an afternoon of fun. I passed Edmonson school giving her an affectionate smile, started up the hill past my first puppy love's house, braked down the hill into Edmonson proper, and since I didn't need gas, I took a sharp left towards the greatest place on earth. The 'ol swimming hole.

A grin plastered my face as I shoved in the clutch, tapped the brake, and pulled off the road into a quasi-parking area. Over the years Mother Nature had filled the creek with torrential rains, raced downstream, changed directions, banked around a corner, and deposited decades of creek bedrock onto a berm. During this process, she hollowed out the bend making a fair-sized pool and leaving majestic trees overhanging the water just begging for ropes that produced daring swings and remarkable splashes.

I was the only one here on this day but the future would see my BFFs, my class-mates, casual acquaintances, and my future husband swimming, laughing, roasting hot dogs, flirting and frolicking, generally care-free and impulsive with that youthful enthusiasm that barricades the past and future, and exists only in the present.

In the future, this swimming hole would rescue me from darkness, become a safe haven and a place that would live in my heart forever.

On the drive home I was relaxed and happy. Water had that effect on me. Our land sat at an intersection of two gravel roads. As I slowed preparing for the turn I looked to my left. Scattered trees dotted the hillside pasture and our house sat at the top of the hill. I wondered what time it was and if I was late. I pushed in the clutch, shifted into low, and began negotiating the turn. Suddenly I realized another vehicle sat in the middle of the road coming down the hill from my house. They had stopped at the intersection as a result of conscientious driving as opposed to obedience to the law as there were no stop signs here in the boondocks.

As I rounded the turn it became abruptly evident that there was no room for side-by-side vehicles on the narrow road. The ditch was overgrown with brambles, limbs, and overgrown brush preventing that avenue of escape. So, I instinctively chose the only alternative and continued with my original intent; I pulled parallel with the vehicle that was so rudely taking his half out of the middle.

My truck sputtered and died. My heart fluttered and wished it could die. My inexperience landed me in my first auto incident. I heard an awful scraping sound as my truck pulled up flush against the interloper car preventing either of us from exiting our vehicles. The other driver looked to be middle-aged, thus vastly more experienced, and probably even had a driver's license. He closely resembled a pan of water on the brink of coming to an enraged boil. I had the presence of mind to put on the brake before I scrambled to the other side of the truck, out the passenger door, and up the hill towards my house while yelling, "Sorry, so sorry" over my shoulder.

I only got a few steps before I saw Daddy Mac and Mama coming down the hill. I never knew if they heard the pseudo collision or saw it. I flew into Mama's arms while Daddy Mac continued to the scene of the accident. My tangled emotions were producing a gully washer of tears. I felt ashamed and remorseful that I had caused the incident, fearful of what Daddy Mac would say or do to me, and sorry for the damage I had done to the other car. The fact that I was an underage driver with no legal authority to operate a vehicle and no insurance coverage thus opening Daddy Mac to lawsuits never crossed my mind.

Daddy Mac drove our old truck into the driveway; I did not run out to meet him. My tears had long since dried as Daddy Mac had been talking to the other driver for an excruciating endless eternity.

I was afraid to look directly at him as he came into the house letting the screen door slam behind him. Mama and I were sitting at The Table awaiting judgment. She was nearly as nervous as I was. I loved her for that. She had not uttered one incriminating word and had instead only inquired as to my wellbeing.

When I finally garnered the courage to look, Daddy Mac's half-grin revealed a general attitude of amusement. Something inside released me, and I relaxed. He wasn't mad. Daddy Mac had apparently pointed out in his rather forceful authoritarian manner that the man was indeed sitting in the middle of the road thus being the sole cause of the accident. And, because Daddy Mac was feeling magnanimous today, he would not call the sheriff, nor press charges, nor insist the man pay for damages to his indispensable farm vehicle nor pay for any medical treatment for his traumatized daughter. The man erupted with gratitude, thanked Daddy Mac repeatedly, started his car, and drove off in a cloud of dust.

CHAPTER 20

"Let us make of our homes sanctuaries of righteousness, places of prayer, and abodes of love, that we might merit the blessings that can come only from our Heavenly Father." Thomas S. Monson

Pre-pubescence has a way about it. One moment it cries and shouts and demands attention. The next it crawls behind and beneath anything it can to escape notice. The hormonal changes within one's body and mind dictate behavior and subjugate any common sense previously acquired.

Such was my state one Saturday morning when I packed my pajamas, grabbed my pillow, sheets, and blanket, and announced I was finished sleeping on the couch. Of course, this bravado was only witnessed by Skeeter; he always agreed with anything I said.

Later in life during my Real Estate phase what I would call an unattached garage sat empty of guests and full of mice beckoning to a preadolescent, discontented woman-child. I felt the ancient call to separate myself from my parents, to strike out on my own, to discover my truth. I went out the screen door being careful not to let it slam. Daddy Mac and Mama were still asleep; the sun barely beneath the horizon emitted just enough light that no flashlight was needed. Skeeter followed behind; his valiant spirit having willed his tired body to follow me into the early morning chill.

The house was constructed of native stone, a fortress of durability, and a testament to Ozark resources. The garage sat as a bookend 150 feet away from the house. The front had a functional garage door flanked by a people door. Through the years Daddy Mac had generously invited his friends to crash there, sometimes overnight, sometimes for weeks. A double bed sat in the center of the room; no one had slept here for ages. Cobwebs clothed in dust laced the windows in each of the other three walls. Debris littered the floor—a broken bristled broom, a rusty dustpan, beer cans crunched in moments of bibulous hilarity.

Quasimodo couldn't have said it better. Sanctuary.

I kicked the beer cans aside, lay my linens on the bed, sat down beside them, hoisted Skeeter up beside me, and looked around. Yes! Yes, this would do nicely. Just needed a bit of cleaning up and it would be good as new. It would be mine. My home within a home.

During breakfast, I presented my case to Daddy Mac. I had thought it all out and had a plan. The extra work to ready the garage for an occupant would be all mine; no one else need add any chores to their own lists. And I would be responsible for getting myself up on time (which I did anyway) and getting into the house, making my breakfast (which I did anyway), and getting on the bus.

Mama didn't care one way or the other; Daddy Mac sat without answering. I waited. We were seated around The Table. Daddy Mac wore his usual work pants with red suspenders—no shirt. A tiny radio sat on The Table crackling out its morning ritual beginning with the stock market. It was literally a stock market report including stock (cows and pigs) accompanied by their going price on the other stock market.

Daddy Mac silently reached for his Skoal can, squeezing a pinch of tobacco between his nicotine-stained thumb and finger. He expertly jammed it inside his cheek while averting his eyes from me. Daddy Mac sometimes smoked and sometimes chewed. Beside the radio that also regularly broadcasted the Kansas City Athletics' games, and sad country Western songs sat cigarettes, a lighter, an ashtray, and a stack of Skoal cans.

Daddy Mac adjusted the tobacco with his tongue and adjusted the radio dial to diminish the static. We listened to the price of pigs, the weather report and finally Johnny Cash belting out Tennessee Flat-Top Box. It was one of Daddy Mac's favorite songs to play on the guitar, so, of course, he waited until it was over. He finally looked across The Table at me. I had been sitting not-so-patiently but wisely keeping my edginess hidden behind folded hands and an impassive face. I waited some more.

I saw the twinkle in his eye before words ever passed his lips. His innate orneriness sparked all around him. He loved giving things to people, and he knew this was definitely a gift for me. He simply said "OK." I jumped up, knocking the chair over behind me, took the two steps between his side of The Table and mine, and threw my arms around his neck. I spent the rest of the day in the garage cleaning, rearranging, and singing and trying to keep dust at a minimum. Skeeter sat on the bed sneezing.

After several attempts at trying to find the perfect place for my first-ever, genuine, legitimate bed, I decided to leave it in the middle of the room. The beautifully curved wrought iron of the head and footboard had been painted white by a previous owner. The chips and scrapes in the paint made no difference to me and would in years to come be quite fashionable.

There was no other furniture except two galvanized buckets. One turned upside down for a makeshift nightstand beside the bed. I laid an embroidered cloth across the top and thought it perfect. The other was discreetly placed in a far dark corner of the room dutifully available if perchance the occasion called for it in the dead of night. A half-used roll of toilet paper sat out of sight inside the bucket.

The unfinished walls of the room were the backsides of the native stone exterior, and the rafter-lined ceiling supported the roof's plywood, tar paper, and shingle sandwich. Nails spiked through at intermittent intervals reminding me of a crude medieval torture contraption. The entire room was ugly as sin to the average joe. To me it was beautiful. As I said: Sanctuary.

By Saturday night Skeeter and I were more than ready to sleep in our new refuge. Supper was over. The little radio was trying to broadcast the baseball game; Daddy Mac kept adjusting the dial. The Kansas City A's were trying to beat the Detroit Tigers; the attempt would prove to be futile. Daddy Mac was certain we would have had a victory if we still had Roger Maris. He continued to grump about losing Roger to the Yankees. The New York Yankees!! If he'd gone anywhere else it might be bearable but to New York! It was salt in the wound. Daddy Mac hated New York. Roger hit 61 home runs that year and was awarded MVP which nearly threw Daddy Mac into apoplexy.

I casually stood up and said good night. Mama and Daddy Mac exchanged silent glances. It wasn't dark; it wasn't light. It was that wonderful time of day when reality gives way to dreams. Where light is so pale you can't quite see where you are stepping while the night silently wraps itself around you.

I grabbed my flashlight and a jar of water. The silence felt fragile; I didn't dare glance around at my parents. Significance saturated the moment far beyond the simple mundane act of going to bed. Skeeter and I walked out the door as if we'd done it every night of our lives.

I opened the people door into the garage and flipped on the light—a bare bulb hanging from a single wire just inside the door. I must stop thinking of it as the garage. For one thing, we had never parked our car in it. I had never even seen a car in it. It had always been a guest bedroom and a catch-all place for storage. Now, it was my room. My bedroom. Where my bed was. My bed.

I switched off the light, walked over to the bed, sat my jar of water and flashlight on the night-stand bucket, plopped Skeeter down on one side of the bed and I lay down on the other. I had assumed I would be too excited to sleep but peace enveloped me almost immediately. I was in my own bed. I was alone. It was so quiet I was almost afraid to breathe. I heard the whipper wills cooing, tree frogs singing and coyotes calling to their mates. I mentally said my nightly prayer and went to sleep.

I woke up with a start when Skeeter abruptly jerked up and away from my arm. I reassuringly put my hand on him for me as well as for him. We were both instantly on high alert. I could hear faint scratching sounds. A mouse? I strained my ears and tried to still my heart. When making up the bed I had the foresight born of country living to assure no part of the bed linens were trailing on the floor. An open invitation to creepy crawlies from the world of insects and tiny mammals. I had not found any mice droppings on the sheets when I began my cleaning spree, so I was fairly certain at least they were not in bed with me.

I lay listening to the scratchings not quite determining the source or location. The sound was quite different from anything I'd heard before and quite unnerving. I was by all accounts a brave girl having spent many days and nights alone and overcome many scary moments. But the mystery of this sound wormed its way into me and stirred up an unfamiliar alarm.

Come morning Mama grinned at me as I entered the house. Daddy Mac sat in his kitchen chair at The Table, cigarette smoke wreathing around his face and up to the ceiling. I pretended it was just another morning. As if I had just arisen from the couch twelve feet away instead of coming in from my own very private room across the yard. I didn't mention the mysterious scratching.

A week went by and true to my word, each morning I came into the house, prepared my breakfast and got on the school bus never once oversleeping. By the next week-end I had grown accustomed to the nocturnal scratchings and deemed it part of the experience of being independent.

Friday night I snuggled with Skeeter beneath the sheet, it was much too hot for the blanket and went immediately to sleep. I was awakened by a new sound. I lay perfectly still and heard it again. A soft plop. Skeeter was already up and had scampered down to the foot of the bed. The scratchings seemed a constant background to yet another plopping sound. I don't know if I heard or felt a movement on my pillow right beside my head. I jumped up, leaned over with my arm resting on the pillow, grabbed the flashlight, and flicked it on.

There, a couple inches from my arm, sat a small brown warrior, his tail curled up and over his back poised for action. Then I saw them on the sheets crawling in a frenzy all over everywhere at once; the sudden light perhaps stimulating them.

Scorpions! The one thing of which I was terrified. The Missouri Ozarks are literally crawling with them and they especially love native stone. The first night after we had moved into our house I discovered one on the back porch crawling on the stone wall. I curiously prodded it with a yardstick and called Daddy Mac to watch the workings of its tail. He unceremoniously squashed the creature flat and warned me to give them a wide berth.

Not long after moving in, I was taking a bath. The water ran while I was in the tub, and I saw a scorpion peek out from beneath the lever that controlled the stopper. I screamed loud and long; Mama came running in thinking who knows what. She never saw the scorpion and insisted I finish my bath which I did post haste.

From that first back-porch encounter to the garage episode, I had been stung multiple times, the sting no worse than a wasp's. I developed an unreasonable fear of scorpions and hated them with a passion. The scorpions were the inexplicable scratching I had heard while they went about their business in the ceiling. Daddy Mac said they probably nested in between the tar paper, shingles and plywood coming out at night to eat, mate and exercise. Who knows why they suddenly decided to dive from their lair and plummet to my bed. Or perhaps they just lost their tiny little foothold.

I grabbed Skeeter, ran into the house, jumped onto the couch, and spent the rest of the night trying to calm down. The couch sat directly opposite the bedroom doorway—there was no door. The next morning Daddy Mac sleepily got out of bed in his usual all-together—Daddy Mac slept in the nude. He wandered toward the living room, spied me on the couch, yelled an obscenity which triggered my own shriek which in turn spooked a scream from Mama who had been blissfully asleep in her own bed.

This early morning episode stimulated Daddy Mac's quick decision to enlist Penny's stepdad to remodel the garage into a proper bedroom before they moved back to the city. I couldn't imagine anyone after living in paradise wanting to move back to purgatory. In my mind, living in the city was a fate worse than death. But then I was too young to understand the economics involved in the lack of employment opportunities in the Ozarks

.

CHAPTER 21

"My best friend is the one who brings out the best in me."   Henry Ford

The big news of the county had arrived. Daddy Mac and Mama sat at The Table discussing the pros and cons of the consolidation of schools. We lived almost equal distances from two small rural town school districts, each of which wanted Edmonson. Daddy Mac had his favorite and never missed an opportunity to voice, loudly, his opinion. In my heart, I voted to stay at Edmonson. I'm not sure how long the county wide debate went on, but it seemed like forever.

Finally, voting day came and went. I don't remember Daddy Mac or Mama ever voting, but that didn't prevent a mighty uproar in our house when things didn't go Daddy Mac's way. His choice for small-town school consolidation lost.

A cold dread settled in my soul. I had memories of a big school I hated. I was an eighth-grader now and could take care of myself, but apprehension filled my summer days and dreams of bullies haunted my nights. Of course, all my Edmonson pals would be there, but we would be separated into our own age-appropriate classes. At Edmonson, we were all together, one for all, all for one. Since Penny moved, I was the only one in my grade at Edmonson which meant no one would be accompanying me to the new classroom. I was on my own.

From an early age I earned my own money but I never had a "job" like most kids. My work was on the small farmstead raising animals. Daddy Mac always gave me a share of any money made from the farm which I considered only right and fair. I worked hard summer or winter, sweltering heat or freezing cold, in sickness and in health.

During the summer before attending the new school, I planned my wardrobe. Some female instinct told me dresses would once again be appropriate. Mama's friend had taught me to sew, but I lacked the confidence of making clothing the town kids would see. So, I chose mail-order. I loved that summer pouring over catalogs and choosing a few dresses my budget would allow. It was the one bright light in the fog of academic uncertainty. I changed my mind numerous times while keeping in mind the deadline for ordering so I would receive the greatly anticipated clothing before school began.

No amount of wishing forestalled the arrival of the first day of school. Now, I would be riding a "real" school bus all yellow and foreign instead of the friendly "woody" station wagon that picked me up for Edmonson.

I could hear it chomping down the gravel road as I stood out in my yard, and just before it reached my house I could see it coming through the trees. The bright shade of yellow seemed to scream caution to me as I walked down the driveway to the road, my new dress swishing around my legs.

The bus ride wasn't so bad as it was full of Edmonson kids. It was when we approached the building and waited in a queue behind other school buses that my stomach lurched. Maybe Daddy Mac was right. Maybe this was going to be a disaster.

There were kids everywhere. I watched all my Edmonson friends go in different directions as I slowly made my way to the eighth-grade room. I walked through the door and saw small groups of girls talking among themselves. I froze in place. The teacher was by her desk chatting with some students. A few minutes crawled by torturing me with every slow agonizing tick. One cache of girls giggled at what I thought must be about me. Suddenly I hated my dress. And my hair. And being there. I felt totally isolated and alone. My cheeks burned and I prayed I wouldn't burst into tears.

A girl in one of the groups looked up at me. She left the others and began walking. I felt my throat constrict. Was she coming toward me? My arms clutched my new notebook; my toes scrunched up in my new oxfords. She stopped in front of me.

"Hello, I'm Janet." Her beautiful smile flashed across her face. Later, I actually thought sunshine beamed from her eyes. My fear subsided; my toes unclenched. A warm sensation coursed through my body. God had answered my prayers. From that very first second, this girl was my bosom life-long friend and confidant.

Janet's world was foreign to me. I was like a little rose whose bud had been closed tight and with Janet's friendship, it opened ever so slowly throughout the next year. Her life was the life of my dreams. Her dad would occasionally have a beer, usually out-of-sight in his den, but he wasn't a drinker. He laughed and joked with us. Her mother was joyful and thoughtful and giggled with us. She sewed Janet's clothing and taught me to make skirts with no pattern. She made daily meals which were shared around a table decked with affection and laughter. She had a little brother which to me was almost magical. And the piece de resistance, they went to church!

Janet became my role model, my best friend, my salvation. She scoffs today when I tell her that, but it's so true. I watched her and learned how to act, how to dress, how to behave in polite society. She didn't know she was teaching me; she didn't know how much I adored her. I didn't realize it at the time, but I took her into my heart as my sister, her brother as my brother, her parents as mine.

I became a staple in their home. I lived to go to Janet's house. From eighth grade graduation to high school graduation, Janet was my everything. Janet spent the night with me twice. The first time was a nightmare. Daddy Mac and Mama were being normal, drinking, and having a grand ole time. Janet and I were to sleep on my fold-out sofa, but there was a problem. The sofa sat in very close proximity to The Table. The Table where drinking, laughing, swearing, and joke-telling were the evening's agenda.

At some point Daddy Mac and Mama left, so Janet and I migrated to the one bedroom. I guess we figured out of sight out of mind. Upon their return, Daddy Mac and Mama came into the bedroom, which had no door, turned on the light, and peered down at us. Daddy Mac kept saying with a drunken slur, "are they asleep? They're not asleep. They're pretending to be asleep."

I was mortified. Janet was witnessing my everyday life. We've often talked about that night; how scared Janet was; how ashamed I was. I cannot imagine the conversation she had with her parents. I was certain that would end our friendship before it got a good start. It didn't. If anything, her parents were even more welcoming. I continued to spend a lot of time at their house, but Janet never again spent the night alone at mine.

The only other time she came home with me was a surprise sixteenth birthday sleepover along with several other friends which included Linda. Linda came into our friendship group when we were freshmen in high school. Linda was an anomaly to me. She came from a Christian school. I hadn't even known there was such a thing. Imagine it…a school that taught about God and Christ and had prayer. I couldn't quite believe such a thing existed and wished with all my heart that I could have gone to such a school. Linda's exceedingly intelligent mind and loving demeanor drew me to her like a moth to a flame. And her penmanship inspired me to a permanent love of calligraphy. Linda and Janet have remained lifelong friends and to this day they have my heart. Whenever I need a good dose of confidence or the need to just feel loved, I go to them. There's nothing like best friends forever.

When Mama surreptitiously invited my girlfriends to my birthday, it was one of my very best childhood experiences. She'd never done anything like that and never did again. I'm sure it was absolutely inspired. I had long since moved from the house to the unattached garage that Daddy Mac and Penny's step-dad had remodeled for me and it made a perfect giggly-girl retreat.

One day Janet's parents drew me aside and said they would like me to come to live with them. My heart was going in two directions at once. I was giddy with mixed emotions. What would it be like to live with Janet and her family? They could be my real family instead of my imagined one. It was sorely tempting. But, in the back of my mind, I saw Daddy Mac's rage and Mama's pain if I were to do such a thing. I couldn't do that to them. I wouldn't do that to them. Not that they would ever have consented. I tearfully declined and asked them to please not mention it to Mama and Daddy Mac. We never spoke of it again. In trying times, I often remembered that offer. It gave me solace and peace and made me feel loved.

CHAPTER 22

*"He's alive? My daddy's alive? I've
got to go find him…"Robyn Starling
<u>Tom & Jerry Movie</u> 1992*

Mama hated housework. Her dishes waited, haphazardly crammed in the sink, beside the sink, spilling onto the drainboard and into the draining rack. Mountains of magazines and days of mail carelessly stacked stood guard like drunken sentries around the living room, staggering up the hall into the bedroom and even venturing into the bathroom. Laundry in the basket, like dough left too long to rise, began its tenuous climb up into the washtubs. Dust added its dim dark dullness to everything horizontal obscuring any beauty within.

    Mama and I had our best mother-daughter moments when Daddy Mac was away on jobs In the winter we made Fox and Goose games in the snow and chased each other laughing, slipping, and sliding around the circle, and then came indoors for hot chocolate and new books checked out from the bookmobile—our traveling library in a van. During summers we butchered chickens, planted gardens and pulled weeds, mowed the grass with a push rotary mower, canned tomatoes, and read. Reading was the one solid lifelong thing we had in common.

Mama wanted to sew, tried to sew but her projects inevitably ended in tangles, unfinished projects, and one ill-fitting blouse. She grew discouraged easily and eagerly discarded her failures for a good book.

There was one household task Mama loved. Making the bed. And, although most days found the bed left in disarray, she occasionally decided to "do up the bed". She taught me the fine art of bedmaking. Popping fresh line-dried sheets in the air to snap out the wrinkles. Smoothing them across the bed and folding them squarely and neatly into a hospital corner. In a moment of gaiety, Mama reached behind her, grabbed a pillow, and launched it across the bed. Finding its target, it muffled my startled giggles and was followed by the pillowcase.

I had just finished making those pillowcases and was proud of my handiwork. Mama, having little inclination to take up needle and thread, was proud of me, too. A friend of Mama's had invited me into her wondrous world of ribbon, embellishments, fabric, and fantasy and taught me how to use them. These pillowcases were blinding white. I had starched and ironed them just so. They had that marvelous little flap tucked inside the opening that hides the pillow—an ingenious clever concept that Mama's friend pulled from her inexhaustible supply of designs.

Best of all was the embroidery. I labored long arduous hours in the flickering dim light of the television while Mama strained to hear the antics of the Andy Griffith Show. The sound was turned low so it wouldn't disturb Daddy Mac dosing on the sofa in a stupor induced by ardent spirits. Mama commented many times that Andy Griffith could put his shoes under her bed anytime. I wondered briefly if anything else could fit under her bed.

By the time I was fifteen I had taken over many household chores, not only because Mama hated them, but because I loved them. It was a perfect arrangement. One laundry day I was putting away the pillowcases. I had just finished the ironing. I loved ironing. Except for Daddy Mac's work pants—they were big and heavy and cumbersome.

Pillowcases, now, that was different. The white, starched fabric felt smooth, pristine and wonderful to my fingers. I thought the embroidery on the pillowcases had an effect so uncommon as to take one so completely by surprise that the breath would temporarily leave the body. A profusion of roses cascaded down the fabric, falling gently over the sides and down around the end.

Not just any roses, WHITE roses. With white leaves and white stems trailing along with abandon. Mama's friend called the technique white on white! How clever! White on White! I loved it. White was my favorite color. Since Daddy Mac never allowed me to wear white I used it in every other project I did. Those pillowcases represented everything I wanted to be, to do. Those pillowcases were me. I picked up a pillowcase and eased it across my cheek. So smooth, so soft, so white.

Instead of just putting away the pillowcases, I decided to clean out and straighten the linen drawer. I began to shift and sort the bed linens, handkerchiefs, and anomalous items when an odd-shaped blue document caught my eye. I removed it from its envelope and read the intricately embellished words at the top of the page.

Marriage certificate. It was Mama and Daddy Mac's documentation of getting married. I smiled. For some reason it made me feel good. A tangible token of love.

I read through the words, the witnesses, the dates. For some reason, I thought of Scarlett O'Hara, Jane Eyre, and Elizabeth Bennet. I think I was born a hopeless romantic, then nourished it with daily reading often with a flashlight under the covers at night and later in my bedroom sanctuary. As I read over the marriage document my mind imagined Daddy Mac rescuing Mama and me from poverty, loneliness, and shame.

Wait a minute. Dates. I read the date again and realization dawned. This was only six months before the birth of my sister, Wanda. I had never thought about it; I had assumed they were married years before.

Tears welled in my eyes blurring the words on the document. For me, this translated into a "have to" scenario. Daddy Mac didn't marry Mama just because he loved her. He didn't marry her to rescue us. He didn't marry her to make the three of us a family. He married her because he had to. He married her because she was having his baby. He married her for Wanda Lynn.

Although it was a good thing they got married regardless of the reason, in my heart, at my age, it felt like a betrayal. He didn't want me; he wanted his own daughter. I know now that was a vast overreaction, but I was an emotional and idealistic fifteen-year-old and already deep in my own version of reality.

This turned out to be not only a year in which my maturity took a giant step forward but a revelatory and magical year as well.

The man's name listed as my father on my birth certificate didn't mean much to me until one late night when my mother made a drunken confession. I was still fifteen and fresh off Mama's marriage date discovery. In my younger years, I was not concerned with birth certificate dad Frank Ewing because he had been killed in the war. Except there was a niggling notion below the surface concerning the date of the end of the war, Frank's death in the war, and the date of my conception. I never investigated, but the shadow of the thought emerged occasionally.

Ewing was a name that kept me separate; I wanted Daddy Mac's name. I wanted to be a family in deed and in name. So, Frank Ewing rarely crossed my mind.

It had been a day of drinking, an afternoon of drinking, an evening of drinking. Daddy Mac was passed out on the couch snoring softly, his toes moving back and forth as they always did when he was in that lovely place between sleep and wake.

Mama and I were in the kitchen alternately cooking and sitting at The Table. The Table that had heard many late-night tales and stories, some of them tall, some of them true, but none of them with the impact this moment was about to have on me and the rest of my life.

Mama began, hesitantly at first but continuing with many remorseful tear-filled interruptions, apologies and self-deprecation told me birth certificate dad Frank Ewing was alive… and married. She refused either by choice or ignorance of the facts, to tell me anything more about him other than his name, possible hometown, Native American heritage, served in the armed forces, probably the Air Force, and married. Married being the operative word here, the barrier to Mama's happiness and subsequently my own.

My teenage emotions exploded. My mind reeled; my heart ripped open, spilling out feelings I didn't know were there. I had a father? A living father? Of course! Frank's alleged death and the end-of-war date *had* come before I could possibly have been conceived. It took days for me to regain my equilibrium.

Once I had my feet under me again my thoughts explored this new person in my life. I imagined a hearth and home full of love, hope, and happiness. Maybe even full of siblings. A haven where no one got drunk, only words of compassion and endearment were uttered, the Lord's name was never taken in vain, and we all went to church on Sunday. My birth certificate dad was alive. I didn't need to be adopted; I already had a father. Frank Ewing. He replaced adoption as my third secret wish. All I had to do was find him.

CHAPTER 23

"Yet each man kills the thing he loves
By each let this be heard.
Some do it with a bitter look
Some with a flattering word.
The coward does it with a kiss
The brave man with a sword."
Oscar Wilde, The Ballad of Reading Gaol

As I grew older, Daddy Mac and I grew apart. I began to resent and hate the lifestyle he and Mama lived. Best Friend Janet, high school, and a new love occupied my heart and my life. Albert appeared on my doorstep one evening to take me skating. I had turned down every request by other boys at school for a date so Albert figured he would come directly to the source, my Mama.

Daddy Mac was out of town working and Mama uncharacteristically agreed to the date. That was the first of many and two years later we became engaged. That was the happiest moment of the life I had lived so far. By this time Albert had enlisted in the Navy and was home on leave. Albert dutifully asked Daddy Mac's permission to marry me and to everyone's surprise he agreed.

Albert had never been Daddy Mac's choice for me; he didn't imbibe, smoke, or visit the local drinking establishments. Albert didn't attend church services regularly but had a firm faith and a generational connection to his church. He promised me secret wish number two, going to church. I dreamed of having a home of my own, a loving non-drinking, non-violent husband, and children. I wanted children.

It was several months prior to our planned wedding and Albert was once again home on leave. Daddy Mac and Mama had tried unsuccessfully to get me attracted to other men, one in particular. They were not at all interested in the social aspect of me being engaged; I think in their heart of hearts they hoped it would be called off. But I was deliriously happy, and I wanted the world to know why. I needed to share my ecstasy with everyone; I let excitement overshadow my good judgment.

I posted our engagement announcement in the local paper.

We were at Albert's house visiting with his mother when the telephone rang. It was Mama. Her demeanor was frigid, but her voice sizzled hot with suppressed anger as she instructed me to get home and get home now.

Grandpa Henry and Grandma Lizzy had come for a visit that day while I had been gone. Albert and I walked into an atypically quiet house. My grandparents were seated in the open living room separated from the kitchen with a wide archway. I assumed a cheery demeanor as I greeted them. Daddy Mac was sitting at his place at The Table; a beer half-consumed sat in front of him, condensation beading on the Coors label. Mama stood at the range cooking; the smell of fish permeated the house. My stomach clenched as I walked over and stood beside her. She ignored me.

I knew in my heart this was about the wedding announcement, so it was no surprise when Daddy Mac burst out with who in the world did I think I was. He ranted on loudly about my self-centeredness and that I had no regard for him or Mama. Periodically gulping his beer and with great animation, he spat his words; they reverberated through my mind, circled around my grandparents and Albert who sat mutely in the adjoining room. They knew anything they said or any interference they attempted would escalate the situation. Daddy Mac's voice lapsed into silence. His rave was on reprieve.

I asked Mama what I could do to help finish up the cooking. She looked at me with a stranger's eyes and told me to get out of her kitchen. Never in my entire life had she ever looked at me with that expression or spoken to me in that tone. It pierced my heart like nothing I had ever experienced. Daddy Mac had never said nor done anything that affected me the way Mama's words had. Every ounce of joy drained from my soul. I was empty, hollow, and cold. I had weathered Daddy Mac's storms my whole life but had never suffered Mama's defection. It had always been she and I against the world. Together we had survived. Now I felt abandoned like she had wrapped me in a blanket and left me on a doorstep.

I stepped to the side of the room and waited. Not moving. Not looking at Albert or Grandma Lizzy. The room was graveyard silent. Normally I would have burst out crying, but there were no tears. I felt dry, a barren desert devoid of life.

The food was ready, and we squeezed around The Table. When we had company, my place was moved next to Daddy Mac. Mama sat directly across from us and refused to look at me. As I started to sit down in my chair, my head began spinning. Albert caught me as strength left my body. The height of happiness I had felt earlier in the day plummeted toward an abysmal dark crevice; the fall seemed endless. A black unbroken pitch into hell.

I was barely aware as Daddy Mac shoved Albert aside, took hold of me, and demanded that I stop it. My body went limp. My head flopped forward, my arms and legs lifeless. I absurdly thought of a spaghetti noodle I had tossed against the kitchen backboard to see if it would stick.

I went in and out of awareness as Daddy Mac dragged me out of the house and onto the porch continuing to tell me to stand up and behave. Chaos reigned for them, but I remained silent in my prison of wretchedness. My heart seemed to literally be broken. It lay in two halves, beating with separation and suffering.

I tried to obey Daddy Mac, but my body would not respond, and it only incensed him further. He dropped me into a webbed lounge chair, old and dusty from many summers on the porch. Mama, Albert, Grandpa Henry, and Grandma Lizzy had followed us out the door. Grandma

Lizzy anxiously asked me if anything hurt. Lying collapsed in the chair I was able to move my hand to my chest before I blacked out. She assumed I was having a heart attack which further added to the pandemonium.

The doctor was called. This was no ordinary doctor. This was a country doctor. For years he had been a frequent guest in our home, a fishing buddy, a friend. He was one of a dying breed of doctors who still made house calls and took payment in a passel of squirrels or basket of tomatoes.

I'm not sure if one can literally die of a broken heart, but I credit our dear doctor with saving my life, at the very least my sanity. Knowing my home situation perfectly, and an expert at handling Daddy Mac, he diagnosed me with a nervous breakdown, gave me a shot of something powerful and announced that I was to be treated with some kindness. He further prescribed that whenever I awoke Albert was to get me out of the house and, of all things, take me swimming. He pronounced that water was the best antidote for anxiety and would release and relax the tension binding me.

I woke up sometime the next afternoon. My grandparents were gone and forever after Grandma Lizzy was never able to speak of the incident. Her tears always came, followed by a wordless hug and I felt her heart was probably broken that night, too.

Mama was very solicitous of me as I lay in their bed and she was hostile toward Daddy Mac when he ventured into the bedroom. Having stayed the entire night, Albert was there beside the bed, holding my gaze, loving and supporting. My body felt heavy; whether leaden from Docs latent drug or just devoid of all joy, I could hardly move.

Eventually, I was able to get out of bed, and as soon as my feet hit the floor Albert whisked me off to the swimming hole. A Navy knight saving his desolate damsel. Just as our beloved country doctor had predicted, the water surrounded me, held me, and coaxed me back into the world of the living. The familiar creek felt like warm and liquid love. It enticed the misery from my body and dispersed it downstream.

I apologized for the wedding announcement; I had usurped a parental right. Daddy Mac and I reached an uncomfortable impasse: he would never stop trying to break up Albert and I and I would never give him up. My life became an emotional tug of war. Daddy Mac continued trying to corrupt Albert's standards even after we were married and had children.

It would be many years before I could forgive Daddy Mac for the lifetime of Mama's emotional and physical abuse. Especially since his tyrannical behavior contributed to her death. Forgiveness would come in an unforeseen and unimaginable way after I found my birth certificate dad, Frank Ewing.

Daddy Mac died the sad lonely death of an alcoholic, a testament to hard living. Now that I am a silver-haired senior I find myself remembering him. As a girl his witticisms were corny and unappreciated. But now, as a woman, I see their value with mature understanding. His lessons were hard at the time, but now I'm grateful to have had a thread of steel woven throughout my tender heart. It facilitated me being able to cope with life's challenges.

Daddy Mac helped shape me into the person I am. Sometimes the road was hard and rocky, but not without its respite parks and beautiful flower-laden gardens. I love him and he will always have a place in my heart.

FRANK

CHAPTER 24

"I cannot think of any need in childhood as strong as the need for a father's protection."
Sigmund Freud

Frank's story also begins on that frigid cold day in the Great Rocky Mountains when my grandfather Robert died. Mama, Emma Eleanor Bryant, had met a military man and now she was pregnant. At least that's the way the story unfolded when it was told to me.

The name Frank C. Ewing printed small and unassuming on my birth certificate didn't have much meaning when I thought he was dead. But, when Mama confessed the true version, that he was very much alive, my world changed.

All my life I had crammed, rammed, and jammed my name, Ida Elizabeth Ewing, as far down the proverbial dank, damp, dark hole as it would go. But now that I knew my father was alive, my focus changed. I had to find him. He was there, somewhere in the world living his life, going about his business, drinking coffee, reading the newspaper, kissing his wife and children goodbye, and going off to a job he loved. The Father Knows Best TV show all wrapped up in my fantasy family.

I didn't know how or how long it would take, but I would find him, and we would be daddy and daughter. I didn't realize it would take a lifetime, but it wouldn't have mattered. I was going to find my father.

I didn't have much to go on. I knew he was a serviceman, but not sure which branch. He couldn't marry Mama because he was already married. Even though he had cheated on his wife, in my mind Frank was not just one more serviceman being unfaithful. He was in love with Mama and returned to his wife because he was gallantly being true to his vows and had to keep his marriage intact. He was doing the right thing.

I wasn't sure he even knew of my existence; to my way of thinking, he was a valiant hero far from home serving his country in a time of war. He had given up happiness with Mama to keep a promise and a commitment he had made with someone else. And in the end he was honorable to his wife and marriage vows. Yes, he had strayed from those vows, but went home to her because of them.

Mama said she thought he was from Illinois…one tiny piece of information that may help me find him.

And, what if he had children? He couldn't very well abandon his family regardless of how much he loved Mama. There was no end to the excuses I made for Frank Ewing. He was my father. I loved him.

If he had children, then I had siblings. My first secret wish!! Oh, the joy this brought to my imaginings. Brothers or sisters, or both; just the possibility made me giddy. No matter that I was no longer a child, my heart raced with anticipation as my search for Frank went on.

What if he went to church? My second secret wish. I envisioned walking through the sanctuary door and sitting in the pew with Mama and my father, perhaps even a brother and sister or two. My imagination knew no bounds, my happiness soared just thinking about it.

And, what if he <u>did</u> know I existed? I fancied that during all these long years of my searching for him that he held me in some secret part of his heart; thought of me and wondered what I was like and loved me as I did him. We could be a family. Daddy/daughter. My third secret wish.

The years rolled on and I had long since dropped the dreaded Ida and went solely by Elizabeth. Then I began using Ewing as my middle name; it gave me a connection to him, my father. I would one day find this mystery man who gave me my name, who gave me my life.

I wrote hundreds of letters trying to find the right Frank C. Ewing. Who knew there were countless Frank Ewings in the world? The letters either came back unopened stamped with an impersonal "unknown occupant" or "not at this address" or the letters were lost in the vast quagmire of the postal world endlessly and mindlessly shuffled from one postal service to another.

I dropped each letter into the mail slot with prayer, hope, and anticipation. Even though each time it ended in disappointment and frustration my mind went forward to a time when I just knew one of my letters would find him and he would come galloping into my life with a father's love.

My life glided through the years giving me three children, nine grandchildren, two great-grandchildren, two husbands, many homes in many states, varied vocations, the mountains, and the valleys of experience. The Lord guided me through good decisions and stayed with me during the bad. Regardless of where I was, who I was with, or what I was doing, that third secret wish lurked beneath the surface. Where was my father?

December 2012 My daughter, Cyndi, had become quite an accomplished genealogist. She caught the spirit of looking for Frank Ewing at a young age and carried it into adulthood. Cyndi quietly and behind the scenes began her own quest of finding her grandfather. One cold winter Missouri day she came to my house and disclosed that during her incalculable number of research hours she had narrowed her long list of all the Frank Ewings who could possibly be her grandfather down to three men.

This was monumental! After a lifetime of searching, scheming, hoping, dreaming I could see a glimmer of possibility. Three! Out of thousands and thousands of Franks. After scores and scores of years. I could hardly believe it. Cyndi only had three names left to research.

Almost as an afterthought as she was going out the door she said, "Oh, one of those three was in prison."

I responded with 100% certainty, "Well, we know it isn't that one."

21 March 2013 Cyndi remained hot on Frank's trail for months. One evening she came over, walked in the door with her computer under her arm, and told me to sit down. She opened her computer, set it on my lap, proceeded to scroll through a series of emails, and told me not to look until she got to her first email inquiry.

When Cyndi stopped scrolling, my eyes scanned an email she had written to a Rebecca Ewing detailing the few things we knew about Frank and inquiring whether she might know anything about him. Cyndi mentioned in her email that she had been looking for her grandfather her entire adult life. Yes, I thought, me too.

My eyes zeroed in on the computer. There in the middle of the screen were words that would change my life:

WELL, YOU FOUND HIM.

Shock reverberated throughout my body. My mouth went dry; my heart pounded. Hot tears blurred my vision. Speech abandoned me. The impossible was possible. The needle had been found in the haystack. My third secret wish had been granted. I had a father. Every perimeter had been met. Every i dotted; every t crossed. Every uncertainty was answered. I had a father.

I read that email twice. Then proceeded to the next and the next and the next. Rebecca Ewing was also the family genealogist. She had searched, found, and loved many a lost relative and brought them into the folds of the Ewing clan. The initial shock of succeeding in the lifelong hunt of locating Frank Ewing never wore off and still amazes me. Cyndi and I pressed on through that fateful night firing emails to Rebecca loaded with questions and she shot them back at us with answers. The emails were like a rosebud unfolding with heartfelt information, pictures, and revelations.

Frank had indeed lived in Illinois. His entire extended family had lived there. My heart soared as my eyes devoured the photographs of a family I had longed for all my life. My father, Frank Ewing was tall, square-jawed, and handsome. His mother, Mable, looked back at me with a grandmother's heart. Rebecca turned out to be my Auntie Becky and she told me that Grandma Mable, Frank's mother, was the essence of love and would have gathered me in as one of her own. I looked into the photographic likeness of Mable's eyes and felt a stirring that rippled through time. A connection that transcended reason. My grandmother. Mable. I thought of Grandma Lizzy and the love she had given me, a step granddaughter, and felt the bond that ties generations together.

My joy was diminished when Auntie Becky told me Frank had passed away a few years earlier. Gone was my chance to get to know the father I had been waiting for. Gone was the opportunity to embrace him, love him, share a lifetime of stories and bask in the father-daughter relationship. The heaviness and profound disappointment that settled in my heart was lessened by the knowledge that we would meet again someday in the great hereafter. The loss of my father was also softened by one of those many emails from Auntie with the news that I had siblings.

Oh, the joy!! Siblings!! Finally, my first secret wish had come true. I had a brother, Jonathan and two sisters, Abigail and Chris. My spirit soared. I had siblings. I was still in the euphoria stage and couldn't wait to make contact with them. My mind whirled, my heart sang, and I couldn't stop thinking about them. My birth family at long last.

Cyndi and I sorted through pictures, identifying family members, thrilled at the fact we were looking at pictures of the long-lost Ewing family. We came upon a photo of the grave markers of an older woman—Grace Lavinia Ewing age 68, a great aunt to me—and another person—Eva Louise Nance age 49. They had died on the same day—March 26, 1965. Cyndi and I speculated they must have been killed in a car accident.

A multitude of emails flowed between Auntie Becky, Cyndi, and I. The evening wore on and ebbed into the first hours of tomorrow. Sometime after midnight, an incoming email began, "I don't know how to tell you this, so I'm just going to say it…"

A heavy foreboding burst upon me. I didn't want to read further. I didn't want the shining that had been with me all night to be tarnished, but I pressed on. As I read the email aloud to Cyndi a great weight descended upon us. I felt my light diminishing, my strength subsiding. I lay my head on the table and let the sobs overtake me.

My father was a murderer.

My dream, my third secret wish, didn't just NOT come true. It was malevolently and with malice thrown to the ground, stomped into powder, and set on fire for good measure.

Cyndi and I were weighed down with the news and bantered it back and forth until we were exhausted. Unbelieving. Unaccepting. Unwilling to let go of the elation we had experienced just hours before.

My son Chad lives in another state, so I told him about Frank's gruesome actions over the phone. My other son, Henry, only lives a few miles away so I went for a visit. Only two words describe their feelings: shock and shock. Devastation and grief swept through the hearts of my children. The joy at having found their grandfather was now shrouded in darkness. It was a burden we endured together.

Chad likened it to when Luke Skywalker listened in horror to Darth Vader's pronouncement that he was Luke's father. When you're watching the movie Star Wars Episode V the expression on Luke's face reveals revulsion at being related to a being who can commit such unspeakable evil. It was incomprehensible that such a thing could be true.

Henry tells his own story:

"I was stacking wood when Mom came over. She had a somber look on her face, and I knew something was wrong. She began telling me about Frank and the terrible things he had done.

"Growing up I had come to know the empty hole in my mom's heart. The hole that held "what would have been". It wasn't something that was discussed—a spoken word here and there, a conversation with a comment all accompanied with "a feeling".

"Over time and maturity, I knew (on my own level of understanding) that this hole in Mom's heart about her father was deep and painful.

"Hearing her speak about what kind of man he really was was hard. My first instinct was to protect her—to convince her that Frank was not her and that it didn't matter. It was OK.

"Knowing my words would never make up for the pain that he had caused her , all I could do was hug her as she cried.

"After she left, I went in to talk to Shonna, my wife. I told her and expressed my concern for mom. I said that I hope mom can accept it, even though it destroyed a life's worth of dreams of the family she longed for."

CHAPTER 25

> *"In keeping silent about evil, in burying it so deep within us that no sign of it appears on the surface, we are implanting it, and it will rise up a thousandfold in the future. When we neither punish nor reproach evildoers, we are not simply protecting their trivial old age, we are thereby ripping the foundations of justice from beneath new generations.*
> Aleksandr I. Solzhenitsyn, <u>The Gulag Archipelago 1918–1956</u>

Elijah Ewing IV is Frank's father, my grandfather. Grace Lavinia Ewing is Elijah's older sister and Frank's aunt. She was a loving, caring, and endearing person to everyone who knew her. She was inherently happy and had a spontaneous, infectious laugh that affected everyone around her. She had a kindness that emanated from her soul, and she shared her worldly possessions with anyone who had a need. For many years Frank lived with Aunt Grace; she gave him a home, loved him, and treated him as her own son.

In 1928 Frank's father Elijah was convicted of armed robbery and assault to murder. A friend had driven Elijah to a café and upon arriving Elijah left his friend in the car completely unaware of Elijah's intentions and went into the café under the pretense of getting some coffee. Things quickly went awry. Elijah pulled out a gun and fired, injuring two people. Their wounds were serious but not life-threatening. He was sentenced to one year to life in Southern Illinois Penitentiary. The wide gap in years, an indeterminate sentence, allowed parole boards to evaluate inmates' behavior and make judgments accordingly. In 1933 he escaped prison and despite using the alias "Carl Evans" he was recaptured.

Years later Elijah's friend and unknowing get-a-way-driver in the ill-fated robbery/shooting met with Auntie Becky. The meeting was arranged by Frank's mother, Mabel. Because he had no idea of Becky's place in the family, that she was Elijah's daughter, he spoke candidly. He told stories of Elijah and relived the days of their friendship when they were making and drinking moonshine. He said Elijah was a great man unless he was sampling their wares—drinking the liqueur they made.

Sometime in the 1930s teenage Frank served 15 months in the state reformatory in Lincoln, Nebraska, and later was also convicted of armed robbery during a poker game. Incarceration was no stranger to Frank. He couldn't or wouldn't keep steady employment and sought after easy money where work was not required. Frank was drawn to the seedier side of life and beguiled women to his own ends. My mother must have been easy prey for him.

I remembered months before when Cyndi as an afterthought said one of the Frank Ewings on our list had been in prison. How sure I had been. How confident that *my* father was not the one locked away from society as if he wasn't fit to associate with the rest of us. That blind and erroneous belief, that daughter's love and adoration, that horribly wrong and mistaken notion was imploding. At first, a tiny undetectable fault, then a growing, spreading, destroying rupture of everything I had ever imagined about my father.

28 Jan 1940 Frank had married Dorothy Doer and had his first child (that we know of) Grace. It is probable that Grace was named after Frank's Aunt Grace Lavinia as his aunt was close to Frank both emotionally and in proximity. As a child, Grace's babysitter's name was Rachel Collins.

15 June 1941 Jonathan Elijah Ewing is born. By this time Frank had divorced Dorothy and married their babysitter, Rachel Collins. When Rachel was eight months pregnant with Jonathan, her husband Frank's grandmother and an aunt came to their home and discovered Rachel lying on the floor. Frank had beaten her unconscious and left her lying in a pool of blood. Frank's history of violent, mercurial behavior was well-known in the family and in the community.

Jonathan, my brother, is deficient in certain mental acuity that most certainly was caused by the severe beating his mother had taken just prior to his birth. He is a kind, sensitive, sweet-spirited man who has always lacked good judgment. Jonathan continually fell in with the wrong crowds. This conduct eventually led him down the path to prison right behind his father and grandfather establishing three generations of Ewings having been incarcerated at Menard State Penitentiary in Illinois. Jonathan's sexual preferences precluded him from ever having biological children thus breaking the notorious Ewing men's pattern of abominable behavior.

1943 Frank and his brother joined the military to help fight World War II. Frank became an armorer/gunner in the Air Force. My childhood fantasy of him being a war hero now had substance. I imagined him in that glassed-in gun turret at the rear of the plane shooting down humanity's enemy.

> *"The soldier is the Army. No army is better than its soldiers. The Soldier is also a citizen. In fact, the highest obligation and privilege of citizenship is that of bearing arms for one's country."*
> *George S. Patton Jr.*

28 May 1944 Frank came home from the war in Europe and was awarded an EAME ribbon with one bronze star, an Air Medal with 3 oak leaf clusters, a Distinguished Flying Cross and ironically, a Good Conduct Medal. He was stationed at Lowry Air Force Base in Denver, Colorado. There was also an Air Force facility in Pueblo, my mother's hometown. It was a little over a hundred miles to Pueblo from Denver, about 12 minutes flying time.

"Never open the door to a lesser evil, for other and greater ones invariably slink in after it."
Baltasar Grecian Morales,
The Art of Worldly Wisdom

1945

Jan 1945 Mama went to work at the Whitman Hotel in Pueblo, Colorado as a waitress. She often talked about her time waitressing. Mama learned the art of interacting with customers and her tips reflected her success. She was slight of build but strong from years of hard work at home. She perfected the balancing act of lining plates up her arm and carrying them to a table. As a child, I watched as she demonstrated that skill much to the amusement of our guests.

April/May 1945 Mama met Frank sometime in the Spring when Colorado is awakening from bone-chilling cold winter wind and breathtaking snow-covered mountain vistas. Easter had just been celebrated on April 8 and exactly one month later on May 8, Germany surrendered ending the war in Europe. Mama still worked at the Hotel Whitman in Pueblo when Fly-boy Frank sauntered in dripping in narcissistic confidence and changed her life.

DADDY TRAILS

The war was over, spirits were high, celebrations continued across America and the planet. Frank had been a tail gunner during the war and tail gunners were renowned for their brave unselfish service to mankind. Their courageous willingness to be in the most vulnerable positions on the planes, reducing their life expectancy to four weeks, placing themselves in danger for the safety and protection of their aircraft and crew secured their place in the hearts of the world's Allied forces. [xxv] And the world's women.

Posters glamorizing gunners were plastered across America and Europe. Perhaps the most famous gunner, Captain Clark Gable, smiled roguishly sitting in the waist of a B-17 Flying Fortress pointing a Browning AN-M2 .50-caliber machine gun at the imaginary German Luftwaffe's Messerschnitt Me 262 fighter jet in the famous "Combat America" recruiting campaign poster.

Although America took full advantage of Clark's military status for publicity, he flew five not so imaginary combat missions, one in which his B-17 was hit by German gunfire severely damaging his aircraft, wounding Clark and two others and killing one crewman. At one point in the war Hitler issued a reward of $5,000 to anyone bringing him Clark Gable. Fortunately, the reward was never claimed. [xxvi]

Gunners were further glamorized by the movie "The Rear Gunner" a documentary-style drama in 1943 featuring Burgess Meredith and Ronald Reagan. [xxvii] Considering Frank's egocentric personality, I can imagine him taking advantage of the persona Clark, Burgess and Ronald portrayed. Frank's natural charisma magnified by the patriotic symbol of altruism depicted by Hollywood made him practically irresistible.

Joe McCarthy, of the notorious McCarthyism hearings of 1954, was an infamous tail-gunner of sorts. "Tail-Gunner Joe" spun his generally safe participation as an "observer" tail-gunner into a tale of heroism which was later proven at least exaggerated or at worst an outright lie. [xxviii] Frank was more of Joe's ilk and less of Clark Gable's.

In addition to employment, 100 fire-proof rooms with radios and culinary services, Hotel Whitman provided Pueblo with nighttime entertainment. I love to dance and so did Mama. The Whitman advertised "Dine and Dance at the Smart New Whitman Lounge Café—

Dancing 9 pm to 1 am in the World-Independent newspaper that covered Walsenburg and Huerfano Counties in Colorado. Cocktails, dancing and live music set the stage. [xxix]Mama fell in love. A twenty-five-year-old dashing handsome hero fresh from the front charmed a hometown girl barely out of her teens.

14 Oct 1945 Frank's Air Force separation date was set. A date that had to have at first brought hope, then grief to my mother. By July Mama knew she was pregnant. I've gone over this scenario in my mind so many, many times. What was she feeling? Thinking? What would her family, her father think? I know from her own confession to me that she thought marriage was inevitable. But, Frank, the master manipulator, had fooled her completely. Not only was he already taken, but he was leaving. For good. Since Rachel, his wife back home, would give birth to his daughter in March 1946, Frank had to have left Colorado sometime in June/July 1945. He probably had accumulated leave as he was officially discharged 14 October 1945.

19 Dec 1945 Mama's father, Robert Warren Bryant dies. His heart was broken; Mama's heart was broken.

"A sociopath is one who sees others as impersonal objects to be manipulated to fulfill their own narcissistic needs without any regard for the hurtful consequences of their selfish actions."
R. Alan Woods   <u>Apologia</u>

1946

1 Feb 1946 I was born. Mama had traveled from Pueblo to Denver for my birth. I always wondered why she didn't stay in Pueblo for her confinement; it wasn't until many years later that I hit upon a possible reason.

26 March 1946   Frank and Rachel's daughter Abigail was born. Abigail and I were only six weeks apart. I imagined I was the goodbye-forever baby and Abigail was the hello-welcome-home baby.

9 May 1946   Only four months after the birth of Abigail Frank was convicted of burglary and larceny. Frank had the perfect opportunity to break with his punitive past and begin his life anew. Instead, he chose the dark path of wickedness that would inevitably lead him to captivity. He served five years of a three-to-eight-year sentence at Southern Illinois Penitentiary, renamed in 1970 as Menard Correctional Center. The Ewing name was no stranger to the prison.

Elijah, Frank's father, was still serving his sentence from 1930 when Frank arrived at the penitentiary in 1946. Prison regulations and schedules allowed them to meet with one another on various occasions. During these sessions, Elijah told Frank about the family rumor that Elijah's spinster sister, Grace Lavinia Ewing, kept cash on hand. She reportedly put it in old tin cans and buried it on her farm. Shortly after Frank was admitted to prison, Elijah was paroled.

Frank's wife, Rachel, took their two children, Jonathan and Abigail, and divorced her wife-beating, womanizing, cheating, lazy, worthless jail-bird husband Frank. Rachel proclaimed that Frank was lazy and could only hold women's jobs and loved being around women more than men because he could manipulate them. The entire Ewing clan supported Rachel knowing their own Frank's psychopathic behavior manifested danger to her and the children.

1946   Elijah is paroled leaving his son behind in prison. Elijah took stock of the situation with Rachel and said that if Frank would not support his ex-wife and children, he would. He rented a lovely large farmhouse with twelve-foot ceilings and eight fireplaces. He moved Rachel and his grandchildren, Jonathan and Abigail, into it. Providing Frank ever got out of the penitentiary Elijah forbid him to see his ex-wife and children, cross the threshold of their home, or ever set foot on the property.

August 1946 Mama quit working at the Whitman Hotel, Pueblo, Colorado; I was six months old.

28 Oct 1946 Mama went to work at the Colorado Fuel and Iron Corporation. She listed herself as divorced with one child. I can't fault her for that little fib; she was battling social mores and familial dismissal. She was trying to make her way in a world dead set against her. Mama listed her home address as 1235 E. Routt Street Pueblo, Colorado. Many years later I would visit that address and stand gazing at the door that Mama had carried me through when it was she and I, alone.

1949 During the time of Elijah's parole Rachel became pregnant with his child... my Auntie Becky. Rebecca was born in August 1949. During the parole officer's visits, Elijah and Rachel hid Baby Becky in an upstairs bedroom to avoid any parole violations. Elijah's parole ended in December 1949.

January 1950 Elijah decided to end his unsavory past when he received his parole. He stepped up and married Rachel. Elijah had three years with his new family Rachel, Jonathan, Abigail, and Rebecca before he was killed in an accident at the coal mine where he worked.

Auntie Becky's convoluted relationship to me proved to be a harbinger of the tangled Ewing family tree. When Frank's ex-wife, Rachel married Frank's father, Elijah, thus producing Rebecca, it made Frank and Rebecca half-siblings, and, made Rachel both Frank's ex-wife and his step-mother.

> *"The conflict between the will to deny horrible events and the will to proclaim them aloud is the central dialectic of psychological trauma."*
> *Judith Lewis Herman*
> <u>*Trauma and Recovery: The Aftermath of Violence –*</u>
> <u>*From Domestic Abuse to Political Terror*</u>

1960's Chris, Frank's first child, and oldest daughter now in her twenties was determined to see her father. Since he married her babysitter, Rachel, Chris had kept him at arm's length. Since Frank had virtually ignored Chris her entire life, that decision had been easy to live with.

Chris found Frank in a bar and attempted to ignite some spark of father-daughter reconciliation. His response was to shamefully and violently attack her and fail in his perverse attempt to rape her. Chris never saw him again.

CHAPTER 26

"Remember that all through history, there have been tyrants and murderers, and for a time, they seem invincible. But in the end, they always fall. Always."
Mahatma Gandhi
<u>*Gandhi: An Autobiography*</u>

March 1965 ˣˣˣ
I was one year into marriage and exquisitely happy. Albert only had a few months left in the Navy and my search for Frank Ewing had been temporarily suspended as I navigated my new life.

Frank never remarried after Rachel divorced him. He bounced around from one meaningless job to another spending a lot of time between said jobs. Census records show Frank as a farmer and living with Elijah's spinster sister, Grace Lavinia Ewing on her farm. He would later say he was fixing up the house readying it for the sales market.

Forty-four-year-old Frank and his second cousin forty-nine-year-old Eva Louise Nance both lived at the farm having been given refuge by the kindness of Aunt Grace. Completely in line with Frank's character he and Louise took full advantage of their adjoining bedrooms on the second floor from which it is believed Aunt Grace was blissfully unaware.

Louise's fourteen-year-old daughter, Sheila Sue, also lived at the farm. Frank's disreputable behavior knew no bounds as he drew Sheila Sue into his loathsome sphere of existence. She had always been a quiet child and spent her time reading. Her youthful innocence was no match for Frank's magnetic persuasion or his evil unrighteous dominion.

28 March 1965 Sunday Evening had settled over the farm just a few miles southwest of Johnston City, Illinois when Frank and Sheila Sue got into her mother's Rambler. By the time they got to Carterville three miles away, Frank was driving in an erratic manner, sideswiped a car, and left the scene. Patrolman Carl McNeal pulled Frank over for reckless driving and through routine questioning knew he lived with his aunt Grace Ewing on a farm. The officer asked about ownership of the car and Frank told him it belonged to Sheila Sue's mother, Louise Nance who also lived at the farm. Patrolman McNeal asked if Frank had permission to drive it and Frank simply said, "Sure."

The officer took note of Sheila Sue; she was a beautiful blonde-haired girl dressed nicely and obviously underage, then asked Frank for his driver's license. Frank fumbled around in his wallet, then admitted he didn't have one. Officer McNeal informed Frank he would need to follow him to the "station house".

When they arrived at police headquarters Frank was charged with reckless driving and operating a vehicle without a license. Frank pled not guilty but being unemployed he did not have $25 to post bail. According to Illinois law, if Frank had had a valid driver's license, he could have used it to post bond and been free to leave.

The officer asked if they should take Sheila Sue home and Frank shook his head and told them his Aunt Grace and Louise were not home, and that they had gone to Springfield (Illinois). The officer assumed they would be home that (Sunday) night, and Frank told him they would not be back until Tuesday.

The lawman was skeptical that Louise had left Sheila Sue in Frank's care. Frank assured the officer that it was quite proper as he was a distant cousin to Sheila Sue. The officers had no choice but to retain

Sheila Sue in custody and they transferred both Frank and Sheila Sue to the county jail in Marion, Illinois a short distance away where they were placed in separate accommodations.

29 March 1965 Monday   Late morning Sheriff Carl Miller questioned Sheila Sue. She was a student at Washington High in Johnston City. Sheila Sue told the sheriff that Aunt Grace and her mother had gone to Springfield (Illinois) to see the doctor, but she did not know the name of the doctor or if he was associated with any hospital. The officers asked Sheila Sue if she had anyone with whom she could stay until her mother returned and Sheila Sue named a cousin who lived in Herrin, Illinois. Herrin was often referred to as "Bloody Herrin" because of the long history of violence in the town. The Sheriff phoned Sheila Sue's cousin who agreed to come and pick her up.

Sheila Sue's cousin was suspicious of the entire situation from the beginning. She thoroughly questioned the police regarding the whereabouts of Aunt Grace and Louise. Later Monday afternoon she telephoned the sheriff's office and said she was very surprised Louise had not called to check on Sheila Sue and that she had tried to call the farm several times with no answer.

The cousin called Louise's employer, John Nesler, owner of the Polar Whip, a local drive-in restaurant, who said Louise had not been to work since Saturday and that he had also tried to call the farmhouse and got no answer. Mr. Nesler later said Louise had been a "very dependable" employee for seven years and that he believed Louise had given Sheila Sue anything she wanted.

The sheriff asked Sheila Sue's cousin if she thought something had happened to Grace and Louise and she said yes and asked the sheriff to please see what he could find out.

Sheriff Miller drove to the Ewing farm and on the front door was a postcard stating, "BE BACK TUESDAY". The Sheriff reported this to Sheila Sue's cousin, and she agreed to keep Sheila Sue that night.

Sheriff Miller began telephoning hospitals and clinics in the Springfield area as soon as he got back to the station. No one had any record of Grace Ewing or Louise Nance.

30 March 1965 Tuesday Sheila Sue's cousin began calling the farmhouse early in the day. That afternoon her anxiety prompted her to enlist the help of Herrin's mayor, Fred Henderson. The mayor referred the situation to Herrin Police Chief Roy Cole. However, since the Ewing farm was outside the city's jurisdiction Roy Cole called Sheriff Miller. The Sheriff then told his deputy, Earl Long, to make a thorough investigation of the missing women. Deputy Long drove to Herrin where Sheila was with her cousin to question her further.

According to Sheila's account on Saturday, she, Frank, and Aunt Grace were home at the farm and her mother, Louise, was at work at the drive-in. After lunch, Frank and Aunt Grace walked out to the detached garage/storage shed. Fifteen minutes later Frank came back into the house and retrieved a suitcase. He told Sheila that Aunt Grace was going down the road to call a taxi to take her to the bus depot and that she was going to see a doctor in Springfield. Frank left the house with the suitcase and returned a few minutes later.

Around 6 pm on Saturday, Louise came home from work and at 630 pm Sheila went roller skating with some friends in Herrin. Later that evening Frank came to the roller rink to pick up Sheila. Sheila Sue told the sheriff's deputy that Frank told her mother, Louise, had gone to Springfield to be with Aunt Grace and they would both be home on Tuesday.

On Sunday, Sheila said, Frank drove her to pick up her boyfriend in Carterville and the three of them spent most of the day at the farmhouse. After they had dropped off her boyfriend, she and Frank were on their way back to the farm when the police stopped them and arrested Frank.

The deputy decided to take Sheila and her cousin with him when he went to the farmhouse to investigate. He asked them to remain in the car while he looked around. Upon seeing the note still attached to the front door he went around and opened the detached garage. The space where the Rambler had been parked was vacant as Frank was still in custody. Deputy Long was a three-year veteran of the Sheriff's office so tried not to disturb anything that might end up being evidence as he made his way toward the back of the garage that was used for storage.

The deputy noticed the outside of the property looked tidy and clean, a stark contrast to the back of the garage. Wicker furniture, rugs, and cardboard boxes were thrown helter-skelter as if they had been thrown there in a rush. Deputy Long stood surveying the unsightly mass of discards as a chill started up his spine. There protruding from under the edge of a rug was a hand.

The deputy carefully searched the premises and determined there was only one body in the garage. That of an elderly woman still wearing her glasses and a little scarf tied around her gray hair. If this was Grace Ewing, where was Louise Nance?

Deputy Long then found an unlocked door to the farmhouse and called Sheriff Miller, Coroner Paul Litton, and Police Chief Cole. Having touched nothing but the phone, the deputy then went out to his squad car to inform Sheila Sue and her cousin. Sheila asked who the body was, but the deputy told them he didn't know and did not disclose his suspicions.

The sheriff, coroner, and police chief arrived shortly and Deputy Long escorted them to the garage. After his preliminary examination, Coroner Litton announced that Grace had been dead for as long as 72 hours.

The three men then went into the farmhouse. Each of the eight rooms was packed with furniture, some of it valuable antiques. Finding nothing suspicious on the main floor the lawmen descended to the basement. It, too, was full of furniture. In a rear corner of the cellar that had only dirt for a floor, they discovered the body of the missing Louise Nance.

What went on here? Grace Ewing was purported to be wealthy, could the killer have been looking for money? It was now dark, and a guard was posted at the premises. Deputy Long drove Sheila Sue and her cousin back to the jail where Sheila Sue was questioned again. She told the same story except she added that when Frank had picked her up at the skating rink he said, "You don't have to worry about a thing. I have taken care of everything." Sheila Sue said she had no idea what he was talking about. Sheila Sue expressed interest in whether or not she would inherit the house and property.

Sheriff Miller did not tell Frank that two bodies had been found at the farm when he questioned him again about the whereabouts of his aunt and cousin. News of the double murder spread quickly in the small community and the sheriff requested that anyone with any information regarding the murders come forward.

A neighbor hearing the request called the police station and said she and some friends had visited the farmhouse around 830 Saturday evening. Her friends waited in the car while she went to the door where Frank informed her Grace and Louise were out of town. According to the coroners' reports, both women were dead by then and the neighbor considered herself fortunate not to have been the third body.

31 March 1965 Wednesday Early Wednesday State's Attorney Kenneth Hubler and Assistant State's Attorney Arthur Melvin went with Deputies Earl Long and Frank Jeters to the farmhouse to execute a more thorough investigation of the premises. The garage yielded a claw hammer covered with what could only be blood.

Sheila Sue's room resembled that of a teenage girl, with a variety of hair, makeup articles, and clothing strewn about, posters of the Beatles rocking the walls, and her clarinet stashed in the corner which she played in the school band.

Frank's room proved to be much more incriminating. The officers found a pair of socks covered with mud on the bottoms—the cellar where Louise's body was found was dirt. A pair of Frank's blue jeans were covered in what appeared to be blood. The jeans pockets contained several items: a copy of Frank's honorable discharge from the Air Force—the one thing in his life of which he was apparently proud, several photos of nude women, and a batch of notes written in pencil.

The notes were correspondence written between Frank and Sheila Sue outlining a plan to run away and be married. Apparently, they had contrived to leave the next week but for some reason changed their minds and decided to go a week early.

One of Sheila's notes stated: "I guess I was kidding about killing her but it's a thought even though I won't try. I can see why you hate her and I do too… I think she hates me, too. If they try to send me up, I wouldn't have the luck to get into a foster home. I would be sent up."

From the notes, the sheriff determined that Frank and Sheila had had sexual relations which was nothing less than statutory rape. They made plans to live in the farmhouse after they were married.

Coroner Litton took the bloodstained clothing of the two women, Frank's blue jeans, and the claw hammer to the Illinois State Crime Lab in Springfield. Deputy Long brought Frank out of his cell for another interrogation and confronted him with the details of the discoveries.

At first Frank denied any involvement with the murders, but after continuous questioning, he confessed. Frank bludgeoned his Aunt Grace to death with a hammer when her back was turned and hid her in the garage. He went to his room, changed clothes, and left the blue jeans evidence on the floor intending to dispose of them later.

Around 630-7 pm when Louise came home from work, she and Frank had sexual relations after which she asked where Grace was. Frank told her Aunt Grace had gone with some neighbors to check on some of her property holdings.

For some reason, Louise went to the garage and discovered Grace's body. Screaming, Louise started for the neighbor's house down the road when Frank persuaded her to calm down and come into the house. When Louise reached for the telephone to call the sheriff, Frank strangled her and took her body to the basement.

Frank insisted that Sheila had played no part in the murders. Frank was charged with two counts of murder and held without bond in the Williamson County jail. Sheila was held on a charge of juvenile delinquency and later released in the custody of her cousin.

1 Apr 1965 Thursday Headlines in the Southern Illinoisan Newspaper read "Ewing To Get Mental Check". [xxxi]

Two carloads of Ewing relatives drove up in front of the jail and Sheriff Miller took extra precautions to see no mischief happened. Frank was driven to the courthouse where he awaited his arraignment in Circuit Court on two charges of murder. He sat in a chair; his hands folded on his lap guarded by Bailiff Sid Dungey. Frank still wore the same rumpled gray slacks, ill-fitting blue sports coat, and striped shirt he wore during his arrest.

Public defender Charles Winters represented him as Frank did not have a penny to his name. Judge John Clayton continued Frank's arraignment until Friday to allow time for a complete psychiatric examination.

2 Apr 1965 Friday Headlines in the Southern Illinoisan Newspaper read "Ewing Sentenced".[xxxii]

Less than 72 hours after the grisly discovery of Grace and Louise's bodies Frank Ewing went to trial for their murder making it one of the rarest cases in Illinois criminal history. Frank solemnly said he understood when Judge Clayton apprised him of his rights. He waived jury indictment and pled guilty.

Assistant State's Attorney Melvin said if Frank had gone to trial, he would have asked for the death penalty. He went on to say, "There is no place in society for this man. This woman provided for him, let him live in her home and looked after him, and he killed her. He slept with the other woman, and he killed her to cover it up."

Frank's unkempt appearance stood testimony to his six days in jail. Gone was the charismatic woman charmer. Gone was the swagger replaced by a solemn countenance and vacant eyes. He stood before the court nervously rolling and unrolling copies containing the charges for his crimes as he was sentenced to a minimum of 80 years with a maximum of 90 years for Aunt Grace's murder. A consecutive sentence was given for Louise's murder of 90 years minimum with a maximum of 100 years.

This same afternoon an ironic swift judgment was meted out. As Frank stood before Judge Clayton receiving a 190-year sentence, a double funeral service was being held for Aunt Grace and Louise. I had seen a picture of this grave marker, two women dying on the same day, and thought it had been a car accident. Now, my grief was compounded.

Frank's hands were placed into cuffs chained to a safety belt and taken back to jail. He would later be transferred to Menard State Penitentiary. Years later Frank would comment that when he arrived at the prison "it felt like coming home."

Frank's psychopathic behavior was immortalized by Lawrence Gardner in Detective Magazine: "Never before had the area encountered such horrible revelations of aberrant, tangled family relationships, of prodigious greed, of unbridled preoccupation with sex and, finally, of sublime indifference to violence and double murder."

Sheila Sue Nance was never charged with anything pertaining to the murders. Frank swore she was innocent, and she had good reports from her school, family, and associates. Sheila Sue lost her innocence to and was victimized by a selfish, egocentric vile criminal.

She stayed with her cousin in Herrin until she was assigned to the foster care system. Judge John Clayton placed her in the home of an aunt and uncle under the supervision of the Illinois Youth Commission. [xxxiii]

CHAPTER 27

> *"Murder in the murderer is no such ruinous*
> *thought as poets and romancers will have it; it does*
> *not unsettle him, or fright him from his ordinary notice*
> *of trifles;*
> *it is an act quite easy to be contemplated."*
> Ralph Waldo Emerson

When I decided to write this book, I asked Aunt Becky for some "good" stories about Frank. I wanted to somehow retrieve a glimmer of that father I had dreamed of for so long. After all, no one is all bad, right?

Aunt Becky replied, "I wish I could contribute some good stories about Frank. I've just never heard any. The truth of the matter is that he was a psychopath. I have stories about him, for sure. None of them you will want to hear. There are so many horrible stories about him, I don't think you want to know. Consider yourself lucky that you are not his biological daughter."

When I received this message, I lay my head down beside my computer and cried. I wept for Frank. I wept for the Ewing family. I wept for my childhood spent in impossible dreams about him. I wept for the years as an adult when I yearned to know him and have a grandfather for my children.

Frank died in prison in 1982 and to the family's knowledge he never exhibited any remorse for his crimes. But he did make some positive strides forward. He became known as "Craftsman Ewing" and from 8 am to 5 pm five days a week he was the full-time instructor of Menard's ceramic program.

I imagine him as he molded the clay into beautiful artifacts that he was also molding his character into something honorable. Seven years before he passed away, he earned a Bachelor of Arts degree. I have a photo of him in his cap and gown solemnly holding his diploma. He was quoted in the prison newspaper "The Menard Times" as saying, "if a man refuses to work with his mind, he can still come out all right by working with his hands."[xxxiv]

28 March 2013   After learning about the murders, I spent days in turmoil. Spinning between hatred and forgiveness. Bouncing back and forth in a macabre mind game of ping pong. When at last I realized it was not in my power to forgive. I wanted to but I just couldn't do it. It isn't that I wouldn't do it, I just wasn't capable of it. That's when I decided to turn it over to the Lord. I cast my heavy burden on Him, just like He asks us to do. I was standing at my kitchen window, looking out on my farm. I was consumed with a great desire to forgive Frank. To forgive him for the darkness he generated, the misery he caused.

"Forgiveness is the fragrance that the violet sheds on the heel that has crushed it." — Mark Twain

Have you ever had the Peace of the Lord settle on you? It's like nothing you'll ever experience. A great calmness, a warm delicious heavenly mantle of love came to rest upon me. It was so sweet and so welcoming, so *forgiving*. I never felt the same way about Frank again. I don't have the tenderness of a daughter's love for him, but I pray for him and love him as part of humankind and a son of God. I still have the grief, but the hatred is gone; vanquished by the sweet spirit of forgiveness.

That incident changed the way I live, and the way I experience life. If I can forgive murder, not just any murder, but the callous cold-hearted act of family killing family, then I can forgive anything.

Daddy Mac swooped in on the coattails of this holy encounter. Forgiveness for the man who raised me rushed in and sweetened my love for him and my memories of him. When I think of him now, I remember the good times. I remember all the wonderful things he taught me when we were fishing or hunting or saving the life of an animal. Gone was any resentment I had harbored in my heart toward Daddy Mac replaced with unconditional love—a special gift from the Savior.

My son Henry related that the day I told him about Frank committing murder he had told his wife, Shonna,
"in some way I hope Mom would turn those feelings of pain about Frank into feelings of love for my Grandpa Mac. He had his issues in life; many I probably don't know about. But he raised and provided for Mom in a way much superior to what Frank could have".
Henry's predictive words came to be.

I realized as I was writing this book that my forgiveness experience happened almost on the anniversary of Aunt Grace's and Louise's deaths. Forty-eight years and two days after unspeakable acts came unfathomable forgiveness. I don't believe in coincidences.

Cyndi, my unrelenting genealogist, came to see me one day and gave me a gift of family so sweet and sublime my spirit soared to new heights. She had traced my ancestry through Frank Ewing to Martin Luther. Martin Luther! He was my 12th great-grandfather, and I was brimming with unbelief. I loved Martin Luther, the father of the Reformation, a great lion of God. I shared his biography with my family along with a small family tree. I was ecstatic. Somehow in the vast realm of reality, Martin Luther in some mysterious way balanced out Frank's horrific deeds. It took righteousness to equalize evil.

After the supreme disappointment and distress of Frank my focus became Frank's one son, Jonathan, and two daughters, Abigail and Grace. I had a brother! I had two sisters! My first secret wish.

My husband, Gary, and I went to meet Aunt Becky in Georgia a few months after I became aware of my Ewing family. She was wonderful. She was a vivacious package of information and amiability. She enthusiastically showed us all her Ewing memorabilia and photographs, told us stories, and accepted us into the family. I was particularly proud of the Cherokee heritage that ran through our blood. Mama had always included Native American in the few facts she had known about Frank. Aunt Becky frequents the annual Pow Wows across America and had many Native American articles of clothing and ephemera which I delighted in trying on.

I was very anxious to meet my brother. Jonathan lived alone in a small tidy apartment with his cat Megan. He was tall, lanky, and had the handsome square jaw of the Ewing men. He walked slow and unsteady, a cane helping him keep his balance. He was cordial but distant, almost as if he lived in his own world. I loved him instantly. He was five years my senior and I realized he could never be mentally or emotionally capable of returning my feelings and be the older brother of my dreams. But that didn't matter. He was in my heart, now. Forever.

Aunt Becky has taken him under her wing and sees to it that he will never be without someone to care for him and love him for the rest of his life.

After visiting Jonathan, we toured further south into Florida to meet my sister, Grace. Except she was no longer Grace having changed her name to Chris. I wondered if the fact she had the same name as Aunt Grace had anything to do with her switching her name to Chris.

What a glorious day for me when we drove up in front of Chris's house. She was almost six years to the day older than me. All my years of wanting a sister surfaced as I embraced her and held her tight. All the Ewings towered over me. Frank, Elijah, and all the Elijahs before him were over six feet tall. I am short. All my children are short. My boys lamented where was their portion of the Ewing height?

Aunt Becky, Jonathan, and a distant relative, Selina Ewing from Minnesota joined us. My spirit soared as we hugged and talked and hugged and talked. Chris was on the quiet side, not shy, just calm and private, Jonathan seemed to be absorbing us a small bit at a time, Aunt Becky was gregarious and full of life, and Selina was fun and quirky. I love quirky. I loved them.

Chris traveled to Missouri some months later and met my family. I was still on cloud nine celebrating the fact that at last, if I did not have my father, I had my father's family. I loved them. Perhaps a bit too much.

True to my nature, I bubbled over with enthusiasm for Chris. It was a bit much for her and true to her nature, in a very serene and unobtrusive way she said I didn't need to text her *every* day. So, we settled into a routine that was comfortable for both of us. Chris passed away a few short years after we met. She will always live in my heart. I love her and remember her hugs.

Abigail, born six short weeks after me, elected not to meet me. I can't blame her in the least. I represent nothing but bad memories and was a living breathing token of Frank's disloyalty to her mother.

Jonathan, my cat-loving brother lost his beloved cat Megan. Aunt Becky said he is now sharing his little apartment with a mean adopted alley cat named Tarzan. As a rule, Jonathan doesn't write much, and that's ok. He will always be my big brother.

I hold all three of them in my heart, and remember them as answers to prayers, as the granting of my first secret wish.

Aunt Becky continues to research every branch of her family, shares her home with her beloved dogs, and teaches in the field of psychology. She credits Frank with spawning her desire to be in the mental health field. We stay in touch through the ubiquitous power of Facebook.

Selina, my lovely, one-of-a-kind Ewing relative, also had a Facebook presence. It was through this omnipresent medium the now popular DNA testing came into the conversation.

PAPA JOE

CHAPTER 28

"Family isn't something that's supposed to be static or set. It's always evolving, turning into something else."—Sarah Dessen

My daughter, Cyndi, our enthusiastic diligent genealogist, had her DNA tested. Lo and behold when it came back there were scores of names of Mexican descent. We just had to laugh because she had researched our family tree through all the branches and twigs, all the twists and turns through the centuries and nowhere, not in the smallest stem, was there even the slightest hint of Mexican, Hispanic or Spanish ancestry. There were only two remote possibilities.

Either Albert, Cyndi's father, who was from Florida, had a stray conquistador or the DNA test had a mistake. Sometimes these things have to simmer a little, so we put it on the back burner, so to speak.

Months later I took a DNA test. I was surprised to see the same Mexican/Spanish names listed. Again, we laughed about it and concluded it wasn't from Albert, it was from me. What in the world was going on? We both thought it had to be a mistake. It just had to be. But a mistake on *both* our DNA tests? Unlikely. For reasons that are still a mystery to me, Cyndi and I, again, put the mysterious DNA findings on the back burner to bubble its way to enlightenment while we went on with our lives. This was totally out of character for either of us.

07 April 2020   What we in my church call the Spirit of Elijah was sweeping the world. Everyone and their brother were getting their DNA tested trying to untangle the complex branches of their family trees.

"Strange, I don't see you. I don't see us related through DNA, crazy!!!" Cousin Selina Ewing wrote to me in Face Book messenger.

Aunt Becky Ewing and Selina had both had their DNA tested. They showed up on each other's tests, but I was nowhere to be found. Her words struck me like I'd been hit with a pillow; not hard enough to knock me down, just hard enough to get my attention. My equilibrium was unequivocally interrupted.

How could that be? Another DNA test mistake? I worked for a couple of weeks before finding Selina's name in Ancestry's system and trying to figure out what was wrong. I also found Aunt Becky's name in Ancestry, and it stubbornly still insisted we were not related. I felt something within me slipping. It was like I was trying to find a tree root on the side of a cliff to hold on to, but there were no roots, family or otherwise.

12 April 2020   Easter Sunday   I felt drawn to open my Ancestry DNA page. I stared at the list of names on the Match List. I took a sheet of notebook paper and wrote the date, "DNA Matches" and began with the first name on the list: "Ernestina Coker". Beside it I wrote "1,823 centaMorgans". Whatever the heck that is.

Then I proceeded to write name after name, filling the paper front and back, double column. I stopped only because I ran out of paper, the Ancestry list went on for thousands of names. (Yes, I counted them.) At the top of the page I wrote: "WHO ARE THESE PEOPLE?"

19 April 2020   "This just gives me a pit in my stomach," I wrote to Selina.

"Me, too," she answered.

"I'm about ready to cry. Don't know how this is possible", I replied.

"I'm sorry I feel bad that I couldn't find you," Selina said.

"I'm just devastated. It took my whole life to find my family, now I feel like I'm being disconnected", I answered. But, true to my indomitable temperament, I wasn't ready to throw in the towel. I concluded with, "But, we'll see."

Selina asked me if I had a Peter Ewing on my DNA test. "I DON'T HAVE ANY EWINGS!!!" I typed in all caps trying to manifest the misery building in my heart.

Quite by accident, I discovered a path to the original Elijah Ewing, Sr—the first of four Elijahs-- born in 1760 that traveled to me not through Frank via all four Elijahs, but through Elijah Sr.'s sister. The little phrase DNA VERIFIED stood beside Elijah's name like a defiant child saying, "See, I am too a Ewing!!"

I screen-printed Selina a copy. It was as if I was clinging desperately to the side of a ship in the middle of the ocean. Elijah's sister was my only link to safely climbing aboard.

Selina replied with, "...prove we are related. Have you any evidence of matching DNA? Anybody can make up a family tree...But, nobody can make up DNA."

I realized at that moment that the ship I was trying to climb aboard was the Titanic and I felt myself slipping away into icy water.

In desperation, I turned to Aunt Becky. Being an academic, she approached the issue logically and with purposeful rational acuity.

"Now, let's trace our steps. What was the first thing that makes you think Frank is your father?"

"His name is on my birth certificate!" I replied with forced bravado.

Even as I said the words, I could feel the certainty of it slipping away. We went through the original facts I had received from Mama and although they were few in number, they were conclusive that *this* Frank Ewing was the same Frank Ewing that had known Mama in Pueblo, Colorado.

A battle began to rage in my heart. DNA notwithstanding there was a reasonable explanation as to why my winding genes did not wrap around the Ewing family and I was going to find it. I decided to take a different approach. I wasn't getting anywhere on the Ewing side, perhaps

I should take a look at some of those scores of names at the top of my DNA match list.

CHAPTER 29

*"The knowledge of secrets is a very enticing
ship, a very tempting voyage."* C JoyBell C

I turned on my computer and opened Ancestry. I hovered the cursor over the DNA tab and clicked on DNA matches. There was Cyndi, my daughter, right at the top. In months past I had searched in vain for Ewing relatives giving this page just a cursory glance. I had chuckled over the many Hispanic names and had even written a lot of them down on Easter morning. But, today, I had a motive. My ancestry was in question. It was shrouded in a cloud of mystery that threatened to upset my genetic applecart.

    Alone in my office, I read what I had written on my paper aloud, "Who are these people?" That phrase had been floating around in my mind for weeks. Perhaps they were connected through the Native American line that ran through Ewing's DNA. My chart showed I did indeed have a good percentage of Indigenous America and, look at that, Mexico! Why had I not noticed this before?

    Ancestry lists the names in descending order of the number of cM present: centaMorgans. What the heck was a centaMorgan? According to Ancestry, "cM (centimorgans): The total amount of DNA you share with your matches is measured in centimorgans (cMs). The higher the number, the more closely you are related."

The second name on the list, the one right after my daughter, the one, according to cM, was more closely related to me than my own granddaughter, was a complete mystery to me. I sat at my computer and stared at the name. Ernestina Coker, who are you?

The computer screen was unrelenting. As it glared at Ernestina's name, I became more fully aware that there was a large part of myself that was unknown. Ernestina and I were connected to one another in ways I couldn't fathom. It was like I had a secret enigmatic closet to which not only did I not have the key, but that I never knew existed.

I bowed my head and said a prayer: this was bigger than anything I could solve on my own.

I glanced at the long list of Hispanic names beneath Ernestina's name. Strangers to me, but linked through centuries of time, attached to me with invisible strands of family connections. I felt as if I was standing on the edge of that cliff still looking for a tree root to grab hold of and not finding it. Going forward meant taking a step over the cliff that might cause me to plummet into a vast unknown and terrifying cavern. No matter. I knew I had to take that step.

On the Ancestry Match list, I scrolled through page after page after page of Latino, Spanish, and Mexican, according to DNA, cousins. I was so unfamiliar with the cultures I didn't even know what to call them. I remembered a mariachi band I had seen when I was in high school. Daddy Mac took us on our one and only vacation touring the Southwest and we dipped briefly into Mexico. It seems a little ironic as my family and I have felt inclined to learn Spanish for several years. We've jokingly said we should have paid attention to that prompting.

I clicked on the names choosing those with a family tree attached. It didn't take long for me to discover they were related to each other. So, they were a family. A BIG family. How did I fit in? I was totally befuddled, but somehow, by the Grace of God, I would uncover how they were related to me.

I went back to the top of the page and clicked on Ernestina's name. Ancestry lists the probability percentage and possible family connections.

For Ernestina and I it was:

Percent	Relationship
100%	grandparent
	grandchild
	half-sibling
	aunt/uncle
	niece/nephew

So, she was definitely 100% one of these relationship possibilities, but which one?

At this point in my journey, I was not ready to give up Frank Ewing. Ignoring the fact that I was missing from the Ewings DNA tests I stormed forward. I knew Frank was my father. My mother said he was, and she should know. Every investigative step I took was from this premise.

So, beginning at the top of Ancestry's Relationship list between Ernestina and me I thought about grandparent. I knew who my grandmothers were: Mama's mother-Minnie Bryant. Frank's mother-Mable Ewing. So, Ernestina was not my grandmother. It was a no-brainer to rule out grandchild.

Next on the list was half-sibling. Hmmm....a half-sister. A sibling! My first secret wish. This took me to the next logical conclusion. While Frank was stationed in Pueblo dating my mother, he could also have been seeing another woman. Since this was in keeping with his personality and track record, I considered it a viable possibility.

The list continued with aunt. With the limited amount of information I had at the time, the probability of Ernestina being my aunt seemed remote, but I jotted it down beside sister.

I ruled out niece mainly because for her to be my niece would take some juggling of family relationships that I just simply couldn't comprehend in my present state of mind.

The next logical step would be to try to contact Ernestina. I had just had those jarring conversations with Selina Ewing a couple of hours before and I was not quite psychologically ready to embark on another gut-wrenching correspondence, but I knew I had to keep moving forward.

Ancestry's page entitled "You and Ernestina Coker" had a "message" button. Like my pioneer grandmother would have gathered up her skirt to avoid the mud, I gathered up my courage and hesitantly typed:
"My DNA test says we are VERY closely related. I would like to pursue this; can you respond? Thank you so much.... elizabeth :)"

I sat there for a moment, my mind whirling, my heart racing, indecision, and resolution wrestling in my soul. Then, instinctively knowing my life was about to, not only change but veer suddenly into a lane of oncoming traffic, I hit enter.

I sat staring at the screen. Surely, I didn't expect an immediate reply, but I felt mesmerized and unable to move on with my day. Somewhere on the other side of cyber city was a woman who suddenly had a place in my heart. I couldn't explain it, but Ernestina caused a spark of warmth within me. This mystery woman who shared family with me, who was a part of the very fabric of myself was making herself known, was heating up a dormant part of my soul I had not even known existed. Hidden someplace in the branches of my family tree she waited for me.

Modern times call for modern measures. I opened a browser and Googled Ernestina Coker. The very first entry said, "Ernestina Coker, Pueblo, Colorado." Chills ran down my spine. I froze. I felt a little light-headed. Mama was from Pueblo. Her whole family was from Pueblo. I had walked the mountain where she grew up. I had watched my children explore the tiny log cabin where she had lived as a girl. Pueblo, Colorado. Ernestina lived in Pueblo. The connection between us got a little stronger.

While I was lost in thought about Ernestina, I noticed a message thread on Ancestry from a year ago that I had completely forgotten about.

CHAPTER 30

*"The truth which history has in store for us
needs to surface someday.
It cannot remain buried forever."*
Niranjan Mudholkar, <u>The Kingdom of God</u>

29 March 2019   One of my DNA matches, Myra Cordova, according to DNA, was a 2nd, 3rd or 4th cousin. She had written me a brief note the year before:

"Hello! Just wanted to reach out because I noticed it's showing us pretty closely related and I was interested as to how? Would love to hear back from you :)"

A couple of hours after her message I had responded:

"Hi Myra, yes I would love to pursue this further. I do not see where our trees connect....do you? So, I do not know HOW we are related. But I'm excited to think it may be through the native American line. That goes through my birth father whom I only found six years ago. So, welcome to my family!!   Now we just have to figure out the link!! My email is *******   Feel free to correspond thru that. :)"

4 June 2019   A couple of months later Myra asked: "Who is your birth father?"

In 2019 I still had the Hispanic DNA matches on the back burner. I still thought it may be an accident (I guess in reality—it was!!)

or that my relationship with all these people was some obscure connection through my Ewing Native American heritage. At any rate, life happens, and I didn't even open Ancestry for months.

26 January 2020 I was shocked and embarrassed that I had let a message from Myra go unnoticed and unanswered for six months. I replied:

"Oh wow....guess I didn't see your msg FROM LAST YR!!! Haha. My birth father is Frank Carlos Ewing"

20 April 2020 A year had gone by and here I was the day after messaging Ernestina. I was reading Myra's thread. I knew Myra was related to Ernestina because under Ernestina's name was a list of DNA matches she and I shared. Myra's name was on that list.

Cyndi and I had been researching and were finally motivated to figure out the mystery of our Hispanic connections. Part of our research inspiration came from the other half of the DNA mystery—why wasn't the Ewing line showing up on either of our DNA tests? So, I decided to message Myra again:

"Myra, Hi!! My daughter and I are working on your (my)line. It looks like you are related to Delores Valdez. I show matches to Ernestina Coker (Delores's daughter). Ernestina shows a VERY CLOSE MATCH--aunt, niece, or sister (half). I can't see all the PRIVATES, so any help you can give me would be awesome--cousin!!! Have a glorious day. e:)

A few minutes later Myra responded:

"Dolores is my great-grandmother. If you would like you can give me a call (she gave me her telephone number).

26 May 2020 I got back to my investigation a month later and sent Myra this message:

"So sorry. I would prefer not to call as I am rural, and my cell cuts me off and garbles the conversation all the time. It looks like Ernestina Manzanares Coker is your great-aunt. Ancestry says she may be my half-sister...I would so appreciate any contact information you may have on her. Also her birth date. Possible?

Myra seemed reluctant to give me Ernestina's contact information and replied:

"Can you tell me where you were born, my family is all from Huerfano County. My Aunt Tina just recently turned 89. Also do you know who your biological parents were?"

I was so disappointed because I wanted with all my heart to contact Ernestina. I chided myself. Of course, she was not going to just give me Ernestina's address and/or phone number. What was I thinking! If I was in Myra's position, I wouldn't have either. Afterall, in this day and age danger lurks everywhere. Myra didn't know me from Adam's house cat. Why should she give me any information regarding her family?

27 May 2020 By this time I had worked out that Ernestina could not be my sister, she had to be my aunt. I had resolved the fact that regardless of Frank's wayward ways he could not be involved in this conundrum of Hispanic connections. From Myra's response, I concluded that Ernestina was called Tina and by her age, she was born in 1931. I reveled in any information I could learn regardless how small. I answered Myra with:

"Denver. 1946. Emma Bryant. Frank Ewing. Tina cannot be my sister if she was born in 1931....my mom was only 6 and my bio dad was in Colorado in 1945. Ancestry says Tina is either my sister, my grandmother, my aunt or my niece!! So I'm guessing aunt.....but how??? Our DNA is so close, only my daughter shows more cMs!!!!!! We have to figure this out....!!!!"

Later that day I sent another message:

"Ok, I was kind of rushed this morning before I went to work. I'm trying to rule out relationships: DNA says she is either my SISTER, GRANDMOTHER, NIECE, or AUNT. So, Tina cannot be my sister because Frank Ewing was 11 in 1931. And, my mother was 6. I know for certain she's not my grandmother.

And, I'm certain she's not my niece: my only sister died in infancy; the half-sisters I found when I found my bio dad are all too young to be involved. That only leaves AUNT. In order for this to be true, one of my grandfathers would have to be Tina's father. My Ewing grandfather as far as I can determine never went to Colorado. My BRYANT grandfather lived in the Pueblo area most of his life. His name is Robert Warren Bryant. He was born in Washington State in 1879 but sometime before 1887, they moved to Colorado because that's where his mother died. He married my grandmother, Minnie Burch in 1920. They had a son in 1921, a daughter (my mom) in 1925, twins in 1926-27, and their last child, a son, in 1929. In 1930 he is on the census as living in Pueblo.

My grandmother died in 1940. I know you are not interested in all that family history, but I thought something may trigger someone's memory from long ago. Myra, I am so sorry as I realize in order for Tina to be my aunt, your gggrandmother Delores would have to have had a relationship with my grandfather.

This can't be easy for you or your family. This is the SECOND time I've been thru this as I only found my bio dad Ewing a few years ago and went thru this same thing. I don't want anything from Ernestina; I wouldn't hurt her for the world. Only to know the truth and to feel that family connection.

And maybe it isn't even AUNT, maybe it's some obscure cousin...!! There are many of your family names that turn up in my daughters and my DNA matches: (I listed several names) and YOU....this is just a few. Well, this gives you something to think about.... elizabeth :)"

OH MY GOODNESS!!!! As I look back on this conversation I'm appalled. I am blatantly accusing her great-grandmother and my grandfather of having a relationship. If someone had accused or even suggested my sweet, sweet Grandma Lizzy of indiscretions I would have exploded.

04 June 2020 Myra simply replied: "I really don't think I can help as I have no information on anything other than they are my family. So sorry if I come up with anything I will let you know."

05 June 2020 I always do some early morning writing on my computer before I go to my real-life job. I opened up Ancestry I read Myra's message she had written the day before.

By this time I was fully and painfully aware of my colossal blunder in suggesting to her that her great-grandmother had been involved with a man in my family.

I saw Myra's indignation between the lines and knew she was done with me. Myra was as politely as possible telling me HANDS OFF my grandmother!!! Through regretful and painful tears I meekly replied,

"I understand…"

CHAPTER 31

"Family isn't something that's supposed to be static or set. It's always evolving, turning into something else." Sarah Dessen

I had tentatively reached out to six names on my DNA match list and so far Myra was the only one who had corresponded with me, and now I had lost her. I was so discouraged. At this point, I was still certain Frank was my father and concluded Mama's dad or possibly her grandfather had initiated my Mexican connection. I didn't know how, but it was the only explanation I could come up with that explained Ernestina Coker being my aunt. She had to be Mama's sister. Or at the very least, Mama's aunt.

I didn't know a lot about my grandfather Robert, but the one thing I did know made me sad. He had treated Mama shamefully when she was expecting me; he broke her heart.

So, it wasn't a leap for me to think he could have had relations with another woman. After all, he had been a widower since Mama was 15 years old. He was lonely.

When I came home from work later on June 5, I rushed to the computer. Lately, it seemed like I was tethered to the internet rummaging and rifling for clues that would help me solve my DNA mystery and bring some rest to my ongoing angst.

I opened Ancestry and read Myra's note again. How could I have been so insensitive as to lose the only connection I had with this new family. Stupid. Stupid. Stupid. I decided to pull myself out of my pity party. This was getting me nowhere. Often when I'm stymied, I turn to my scriptures. I opened to Daniel 5:12 and the words" dissolving doubts" leaped out at me. I needed to start having faith that God would open up a way and stop doubting that my DNA dilemma would be solved.

I went back to my computer and clicked over to Facebook. There was a new message that had been written the day before, June 4, the same day Myra wrote her last message to me. It was from someone named Randy Randy. I wasn't friends (on Facebook) with a Randy.

He said ,"Hello, I am related to you through AncestryDNA!! Just wanted to reach out..."

I'm very cautious about who I "talk" to on Facebook. Who was this person? I decided to message him on Ancestry instead of Facebook.

"I received a note on Messenger from Randy Randy....was that you? I can't seem to access it again.... Your tree is locked so I cannot see HOW we are related... through Bryant? Manzanares? Ewing? Have a good day.... e:)"

For some reason after I had read Randy Randy's message on FB and closed it, I couldn't get back to it. Electronics have a mind of their own around me. I've had more than one IT person tell me, "well, I've never had *that* happen before!" So, I'm used to bizarre computer goings on.

Later in the day, I was able to open Randy Randy's message and from there went to his Facebook profile. His page snapped into being. My eyes grew large, a smile was afraid to form on my lips and I held my breath. He looked Hispanic. Could it be? I scrolled down to his friends and there they were. My DNA cousins were all over his friend list. I read over the names through my tears, yes, there was Myra, devoured their faces and felt the strand of DNA tightening around my heart. I had found them!

And, pièce de résistance…Ernestina Coker smiled out at me from her Facebook page. I looked unbelievingly into her eyes. She seemed to be claiming me; distance and time did not exist. She was beautiful. Ernestina…Aunt Tina. Tia Tina. The Spanish word for aunt just popped into my head. She was my Tia Tina. I didn't know how, but at this moment that was irrelevant. There she was, in the flesh. Her image seared into my mind.

07 June 2020 I didn't see Randy's reply until two days later, but he had replied a couple hours after I reached out. "Yes, that's me! I would be related through Manzanares/Valdez."

So, my eyes had not deceived me while looking at his photos on Facebook. He was in the Manzanares line. I replied,

"Oh HI cuz!! I'm trying to find information on Ernestine Coker. She's a Valdez/Manzanares. Her DNA is CLOSE to me…2nd only to my daughter! Are you willing to link your tree ? I see a lot of cousins who took the DNA test!! So you and I are cousins..1st or 2nd!!? All of my mother's family are from the Pueblo area."

I also asked him if he was related to one of the names on my DNA match list, Antoinette Moore, and it turns out that it was his mother and he explained their relationship to Tia Tina.

I was beyond excited that he was so closely related to Tia Tina and realized he most likely had her contact information. I replied:

"Oh my goodness!!!! Because Ancestry says Ernestine is either my half-sister -- which I have ruled out-   - or my AUNT. I would dearly love to communicate with her...is that possible??"

Hold on…he was no more likely to hand me that information than Myra was.

From Randy: "I can tell you that I will call and tell her about it...do you have a number I can share with her? How did you rule out half-sister? You have me interested now... How many cM's do you share with Ernestine?"

I wasn't really expecting him to give me her number, but I had to ask. At least he said he would talk to Ernestina about me. That was a giant leap forward. I eagerly composed my answer and tried to explain how I had arrived at my conclusions.

" My heart is pounding. I share 1823cMs with Ernestine. Ok...when Ernestine was born (I think 1931?)   My birth father (now there's a story) was 11 and my mother (1925-1995) was 6..so she can't be my sister. SHE HAS TO BE MY AUNT... which means Doloritas had a relationship with my mother's father ROBERT WARREN BRYANT. (1879-1945) Like I said...my mother's family are all from Colorado...Pueblo and surrounding areas.

I completely understand the shocking nature of this. Perhaps you, your mom or someone else in your family would rather talk to Ernestine. It's just that I have this CONNECTION to her in my heart and long to know her. BUT IF SHE DOESN'T WANT TO DEAL WITH THIS I TOTALLY UNDERSTAND."

I gave him all my contact information.
He immediately responded.
"Ok, I will try and contact her. I can tell you, Doloritas, is my Great Grandma, Ernestine's mother. I will let you know...how interesting!"

I replied, "Well cousin, you rock! Thank you so much!!! Have a MONUMENTAL day. :)e"

Now we were getting somewhere. I just knew if Randy spoke with Ernestina we could clear this up. Surely, someone, sometime, somewhere had heard the name Robert Bryant. Surely, we would discover that Tia Tina (Ernestina) was my mother's sister and I could know for certain that she was my aunt.

I let my emotions run away with me. I thought about all those Mexican faces, they were mine! DNA said so. They were cousins, first, second, third and fourth. I couldn't stop myself from clicking from one to another on Facebook. There were so many! I absolutely loved it. One thing became patently obvious, they loved each other. They supported one another on special days, like birthdays or graduations or new jobs. And it didn't matter how far "removed" down the family line they were, everyone still joined in the well-wishing.

And, they had family reunions! One year they had t-shirts made announcing their family name and the year. Another year they all wore Christmas plaid. Oh my gosh when I saw that picture-perfect-plaid it just made me cry. They were so beautiful and smiling and together.

I wasn't sure how I fit in, but my heart told me I did.

09 June 2020 Randy and I switched from Ancestry messenger to texting. He began sending me pictures, lots of pictures. I ate them up! It was like nourishment to my starving soul. At this time I'm still thinking Ernestina's father is my grandfather, Robert, making her Mama's sister and my aunt.

Randy and I traded answers and questions all day each time he sent more photos. My heart was flying; I felt so happy. Randy made his Ancestry tree public for a little while for me to take a look at. I poured over it looking at his ancestors…MY ancestors. If a person is still living their name does not appear in Ancestry, it just says PRIVATE. So, I started trying to match all the PRIVATEs with the names on my DNA match list. It was impossible.

Then, at 11:11 pm Randy texted me:

"That (Ernestina being Robert's daughter) couldn't be possible from my end because Ernestina's DNA verifies that her father was Antonio (Manzanares, Sr) based off accounts of several family members…she doesn't have a lot of England/Wales, which would be representative of Robert being her father…"

Then a minute later he texted: "She doesn't have any England/Wales".

I immediately replied, "Oh!!! Well if Antonio is her father, then she has to be my aunt some other way..."

My brain felt like I had literally run into a brick wall. I felt blindsided, dazed and confused. What? The only thing I could think of was to go back to Frank being in Colorado at the right time to have fathered a girl-child...maybe Ernestina had a sister who was my aunt.

Ernestina's only sister could not have been Frank's daughter...the dates he was in Colorado just didn't allow it.

Randy was confused. I was confused. Finally, still stubbornly holding to the Frank/Robert scenario, I said,

"Maybe you'll have to take the name of Frank Ewing and Robert Bryant and ask everyone in your family if they've ever heard either one of those names! Because my connection to you has to be through one of these men: my grandfather or my father. I can't figure out any other way we could be connected."

Randy replied, "I'll check it out, work in progress!!"

By this time it was 11:51 pm. I closed by saying:

"Thanks for hashing this out with me, Randy. I really appreciate it. I have to call it a night. Rest well and be safe out there. ☐ zzzzzzzz"

He closed with "Thanks, you too."

The be safe references referred to COVID 19 still lurking everywhere.

It was 11:55 pm. Almost midnight. I was so frustrated. That happens when you keep trying to shove a puzzle piece where it doesn't fit. I couldn't sleep. I kept devising possible scenarios over and over until my head was spinning, my heart was aching, and my soul was searching for something I knew not what.

Bewilderment abounds. Every circumstance I could come up with could not be even remotely possible. And, yet, it was not only possible, it was fact. I was connected to Ernestina and this family in some unfathomable way. There was only one thing left to do: call my daughter, Cyndi. I knew she was up as she had texted a few times during my conversation with Randy.

I pushed her name button on my phone and waited…and waited for the call to go through. We're in the country and it takes its sweet time to connect, sometimes it doesn't connect at all and when it does sometimes it cuts you off right away or just makes the conversation annoying by not letting you hear half of what the other person is saying.

Finally Cyndi answers. I pour out my heart relaying Randy and I's conversation emphasizing that Ernestina cannot possibly be Grandpa Robert's daughter. And, Frank, for once in his life, cannot be the culprit as he wasn't in Colorado at the right time. *There just isn't any other way. How can I possibly be related to Ernestina?*

> *"With a secret like that, at some point the secret itself becomes irrelevant.*
> *The fact that you kept it does not."*
> Sara Gruen, <u>Water for Elephants</u>

10 June 2020 It was seconds to midnight. Cyndi paused. I'll always remember that pause.

"Mom, listen to me. There *is* another way. It's not your grandpa Robert. It's not Frank. It's your mom."

I swear I could hear some immortal clock in the heavens striking midnight as that last puzzle piece slid into place. *My mom??? My mom?!* My mother had the relationship?

I felt dizzy and hot. I couldn't get my breath. My Mom? You know how a concept can come to you all at once? Like a sudden understanding of the inner workings of algebra. Like the knowledge of exactly what your cat is thinking. I felt like someone had hit me in the chest with a two-by-four as that hypothesis drifted down into my psyche. My mom. It was my mom.

I was shocked, dismayed, and disoriented. My whole world changed. If it was Mama, that meant Frank Ewing was not my father. An entire lifetime of wondering about him, thinking about him, searching for him, finding him coalesced into a ball and exploded. My world shattered into a million fragments crushing my heart into splinters of unbelief.

I felt betrayed, deserted, and deceived. In addition to Frank not being my father, Mama had lied to me. Or, at the very least withheld pertinent information. I remembered the night she told me Frank had not been killed in the war. That he was married. How I knew in that moment we would never be a family, but at least I knew he was alive. And, if Frank was alive, I could find him and know him. But now, everything Mama had told me was a lie. She lied not just that night, but years of silence testified of her betrayal to me. Frank was not my father. If he wasn't my father, *who was?*

Cyndi waited on the other end of our phone conversation. I croaked out the words,

"My mom? No, it can't be."

My mind was rejecting this new impossible notion, but my heart had already accepted it. Somewhere within the corridors of myself, the truth echoed loud and clear. Frank Ewing was not my father. This new concept left a hollow gaping hole in my center. A vacuum that already cried to be filled.

As gently as one can destroy and dismantle a belief that was a lifetime in the making, Cyndi continued in her systematic way to explain how she had come to this conclusion. It was simply a matter of DNA. We shared Ernestina's Mexican blood and she did not have any of Grandpa Robert's European blood. Therefore, it was impossible for Grandpa to be involved. That only left Mama as the solution. Mama had a relationship with someone other than Frank. Someone in Ernestina's family. And, if Ancestry was correct and she was my aunt, it had to have been Ernestina's brother. There was a remote possibility it was her father, but we ruled that out as age and the timeline just didn't fit.

My mind raced with options. I thought of the DNA Match list. I didn't think Ernestina had a brother listed. I conjured up more months of endlessly searching the corridors of family history and cringed. Then I thought of Randy, he could help me name Ernestina's brothers. But, of course, Cyndi, my personal genealogist, had already researched their family tree.

Cyndi's next words entered my mind, not like a frozen juggernaut steamrolling over me, but like a soft warm breeze whispering truth.

"Antonio Jose Manzanares, Jr. I think your dad's name is Antonio Jose Manzanares, Jr."

The name penetrated my being. A kaleidoscope of feelings engulfed me; they swarmed throughout my body buzzing with the veracity of a new father. I was hot. I was cold. I was happy. I was terrified. I was mad. My brain swirled with memories of all those sweet and happy faces I had seen on Facebook. I remembered the name Manzanares multiple places on my Match List.

Cyndi and I spent some time hashing and rehashing this new development. By this time it was 1:30 am so we called it a day. As soon as we hung up, I burst into tears. Not just tears, sobs. I gave in to what I do in times of calamity. I laid my head on my desk and cried my heart out.

I cried for myself: the little girl who had longed for a father and who had harbored her third secret wish. I cried for the young woman who vowed to find him one day. I cried for the mother who wanted her children to know their grandfather. I cried for the daughter whose mother had perpetuated a lifelong lie.

When the tears finally stopped and instead of bitter empty memory, I was filled with an embryo of joy. An invisible warmth embraced me, comforted me, and bore testimony of this new truth. I felt God confirming that Antonio Jose was my father.

My name was Manzanares.

I immediately opened not only Ancestry but my other genealogy website, Family Search. I added Antonio Jose Manzanares, Jr as my father. Then I just sat and stared at my family tree on the screen. Hope glimmered within me. I had enough of his family names that I knew I would be able to discover what he was like, and who he was as a person. I thought of Frank Ewing and the unimaginable horrific skeleton I had found in his closet. I seriously didn't know if I could handle another emotional episode like that.

I put the situation in God's hands, looked at the time, and turned off my computer. It was 3 am.

I tried to sleep, but it was far from me. I had what I call monkey brain; it kept thinking about my new father until the birds began to sing the sun up. I had to go to work, but before I did, I texted Randy. I wanted him to know about our discovery and conclusion. And, because I didn't want him to freak out if he saw it, I told him I had changed my father's name in Ancestry. I hoped he wouldn't think that a presumption; I had a fear that he might. I didn't want to ruin relationships before they even had a chance to grow.

I told Randy we had two possibilities: Ernestina's brother or her father. But, since I had entered the brother into Ancestry as my father, he was obviously my candidate. I didn't mention the affirming experience God had given me. I held my breath, hit send, and went to work. Would Randy think this was crazy?

"Isn't it astonishing that all these secrets have been preserved for so many years just so we could discover them!" Orville Wright

It was a long emotional day for me. I was tired physically, mentally, and psychologically. In a couple of days it would be one of my grandson's birthday; a grandson who had gone to live with the Lord at age 10, my sweet Zakk. I always carried him in my heart, especially on his birthday week.

Today someone new was in my heart, my father. In fairness to my employer, I always try to keep my mind on my work while I'm there. It was exceptionally hard that day.

As soon as I got off work, I clicked on my phone and checked my texts. There was Randy. Bless his heart, he had texted just ten minutes after receiving my message that morning.

"lol, my wife and I came to the same conclusion...We also think it was my Uncle Tony...We'll talk later. You're family either way!!!"

My tears came. Again. They had been coming all day at the least provocation. Randy and his wife had discussed it. For some reason that made me feel loved...included. Uncle Tony. I loved that. His family and friends called him Tony. It was the first bit of information I had about my father.

I spent a few days walking the tightrope of emotions; trying to balance who I was with this bombshell information. Tears flowed from a place I hadn't realized still existed. An unexplored, unknown corner of myself where all the dreams of having my own father had been stored. Where my secret wish number three lay broken and abandoned. I was overwhelmed with being part of a family I knew nothing about. It was a new experience, a new culture, and a new way of looking at myself. My lifelong third wish slowly began to reassemble. Hope was only a bud, but it was there.

All the doubts about my origin I had experienced when I found the Ewings surfaced. I was, as Mama used to say, from the wrong side of the blanket. Why would this new family want anything to do with me? Why would they even acknowledge me? My presence, my very existence would conjure unknown and unwanted feelings. I would disrupt memories and disturb relationships causing turmoil, confusion, and perhaps even anger.

I thought of Myra's reaction to my thoughtless and erroneous hypothesis that her great grandmother Doloritas Maria (now my grandmother!) had loved someone else besides her husband (my grandfather!). I did not want to elicit those kinds of feelings in this new and wonderful family.

I looked at their Facebook faces a dozen times during these confusing days and each time I loved them more. Each time I wanted to be in their family circle. I wanted to be a part of their obvious love and inclusion. That yearning was expressed in the fountain of tears that for days just kept flowing.

13 June 2020 Myra came forward with conversation and many, many pictures. I spent the day receiving, saving, and savoring photos of my father, my grandparents on both sides, cousins, and more cousins. I absolutely loved it. I especially loved that Myra had seemingly forgiven me for suggesting that my grandmother, her great-grandmother, Dolorita, had done anything untoward. I reveled in being a part of this marvelous family. My love for them grew exponentially as the photographs poured through the internet.

Myra was most gracious but warned me to tread carefully. Tony Joe's wife was still living, and she is a beloved member of the family. Everyone, rightfully so, was solicitous of her feelings. I would never ever intentionally hurt her. My heart warmed toward her, the woman who loved my father, who bore his children, who knew him better than anyone on earth. I longed to hold her in my arms and be a daughter she never had.

27 June 2020 Of course, almost from the first moment I heard my father's name, another thought came spontaneously. It burst forth in tandem with Tony from the corner where my dreams are stored. The question that is inseparably connected to my biological father surfaced and kept surfacing until I paid it heed. My first secret wish. Do I have siblings?

My heart leapt as I learned that Tony had three sons. I had, not one, but three brothers. As soon as I learned they existed I went in search of them—I could not restrain myself. Of course, they were younger than I am, so I had to adjust my mental position to being a big sister. I thought of Jonathan Ewing with love. He will always be my big brother—DNA notwithstanding.

I learned one brother had died and found another brother on Facebook. He had more than one account and it was obvious he rarely used them. I wondered whether to contact not only him but several names who were in the Manzanares family who were also recorded on my Ancestry Match List.

How does one announce her presence, her very existence to a family who never even had the thought that one of their own had an unknown daughter? An out-of-wedlock child. It was a bombshell that could produce terrible consequences, that could destroy treasured memories, and that could inflict pain and heartache.

Because their warm and loving relationships with one another were blatantly obvious on Facebook, I knew the ripples of my announcement would quickly flow throughout the family circle. Would it cause bewilderment, confusion, or even anger? For me, it was like standing before a door wondering who would emerge, The Lady or The Tiger? I thought of the possibility of them accepting me. The joy that flooded into my heart answered my question. I would open that door.

I composed a message and sent duplicates to my first cousins, plus, of course, Myra. I Googled my brothers and sent both snail-mail letters.

Then, I waited. It wasn't long before responses began coming from cousins. We arranged a Zoom meeting for July 12 which I looked forward to with trepidation. I wanted to meet them, but at the same time, I was afraid they would reject me to my face. Would they deny my relationship? Would they disparage my mother? Would I be a cast-off? I most of all wanted to meet Ernestina. What would she think of me? She was reaching to me through time, a stranger bound to me with genetic cords of family.

What an emotional day for me when I shared with my sons, Chad and Henry, my implausible, improbable, incredible news of having yet another father. A third father. This time a real bonafide blood-related DNA-proven father. This time a forever father. They took it in good stride, both actually relieved not to have a rapist and murderer as a grandfather. Both were relieved not to have the vicious and violent Ewing bloodline flowing through them.

Several of us had noticed Henry's uncanny resemblance to Papa Joe. Henry took separate photographs of him and Papa Joe and Photo Shopped them to show the left side of Henry's face to the right side of Papa Joe's. And then the right side of Henry to the left side of Papa Joe. An incredible match!! The result left little doubt in anyone's mind as to whether they are related!

In Henry's words:
"A few years after learning about Frank, Mom again came over to talk. Unlike Frank's story, this time she had an air of joy as she began telling me the story. She and my sister, Cyndi, had been on quite a journey!

"That journey had people in it that were mysterious. Those mysteries were family. A loving family. I cannot really articulate the feelings I have. No longer do I have to be stoic and tell myself and my mom that her father and his acts are a million miles away. They are not.

"Instead, they have filled up the empty hole past the level of her youth. Her heart is now mended, if scarred, and fuller than it has ever been. Returning her to the idea "of what might have been."

Henry was right. My heart was mended. I ended my new father narrative with, "Oh, and by the way, we're Mexican!"
For some reason, that revelation brought joy, smiles, explicable happiness of the heart and a shared sentiment of "Oh my goodness, we should have learned Spanish!!"
Henry smiled and said, "Does this mean we have to give up Martin Luther?"

CHAPTER 32

"Few people dare now to say that two beings have fallen in love because they have looked at each other. Yet it is this way that love begins, and in this way only."
Victor Hugo   <u>Les Miserables</u>

2 July 2020   As I so often did, I was browsing through Ancestry when I happened upon a hint for Mama. I clicked the little green leaf and made an exciting discovery. I was about to unearth a missing link.

The hint was an employment application for my mother when she went to work for the Colorado Steelworks as a waitress. The date was October 28, 1946. I was eight months old; Mama was 21 years. She had been just 20 years old when I was born. I smiled as I read the application; it was clinical and cold, but it elicited a warm sensation within me.

The document proclaimed Emma Eleanor Bryant was an American citizen, born in Pueblo, Colorado, and currently lived at 1235 E. Routt. She had hazel eyes, was 5' 4", and weighed a scant 108 pounds. Mama always was a wee girl. It didn't list her hair color, but she always described herself as being a dishwater blonde. I never thought that did her justice. I thought she was beautiful, and I have a photo of her posing in a bathing suit where she had won second place in a beauty contest. Mama didn't have much to brag about in her younger days so that photo was a symbol of success for her. I still display it proudly in my home.

The employment record stated that Mama completed eight years of grammar school, two years of junior high, and started but did not finish one year of high school. That corresponded with the account Mama had told me. She quit her freshman year when her mother died to be the mother of the household; to be a mother to her siblings and a housekeeper for her father.

The record listed "number of children under 16" as one. Me. For some reason that brought tears. It was just Mama and me. She was truly alone battling societal mores that waged a silent war against unwed mothers. It is no wonder that under the choices of "Single, Married, Separated or Divorced" the typist marked an "x" under the "Yes" column beside "divorced". I did not fault Mama for this little lie. She was doing what she could to make a living for us. To feed us, house us, and clothe us. Years later when I had children of my own, Mama's brother, Uncle Bobby visited me and described Mama's closet. There on the closet rack were very few dresses for her, but several little dresses for me lined up as a testament of love and sacrifice.

At the bottom of the Ancestry document was Former Work History – Name and address of employer: Whitman Hotel, Pueblo, Colorado; 1/45 to 8/46. It's amazing how the smallest seemingly inconsequential bit of information can turn out to be of the utmost importance. I knew Mama had been a waitress at a couple of places while we still lived in Colorado. Amazingly enough, Mama had saved several cute little aprons from her waitressing days that I had been enamored of as a child.

I immediately Googled Whitman Hotel. It was a new "Commercial Hotel" with "100 Modern Fireproof Rooms" going for "$1.50, $2.00, $2.50" a night. It was also a "NO UPS", whatever that means! It sported a coffee shop and a "Whitman Lounge Café" in which I envisioned Mama waitressing in her usual perky style.

Mama worked at the Whitman during my conception and birth until I was six months old. Could this be where she met my father? Had

Antonio worked there as well? I had spent many hours pondering the improbability of how they came to know one another. She was Scotch/Irish/English; he was Mexican. She was 19 when she first started at Whitman; he was 15. She was protestant; he was Catholic. They were separated by the impossible impenetrable gulf of race, age, and religion. Each one was individually unfeasible in 1946; together these obstacles presented a mountain of resistance and multiplied the unlikelihood of them ever having had a relationship. And yet they did.

12 July 2020   When at last the Zoom Day came, it was like a birthday. My excitement could hardly be contained. I started the zoom and waited. One… two cousins came on…then three and finally four. Four beautiful faces. Four new lives came into my life: Antoinette, Renee, Marla, and Randy. One of my sons and his wife, Chad and Kerrie, tried to join in but never quite got it to work; we only caught sight of their faces for a few minutes, and then they were gone.

I was so happy to see Randy and drank in his beautiful smile and kind eyes. He had a persona of niceness that transcended electronic media and penetrated my heart. He had been so kind to help me in my journey and I will always love him for that. Randy's mother, Antoinette, is my first cousin making Randy a cousin once removed, but I love him more than that. Is it wrong to wish he is my brother?

Randy's mother, Antoinette, and two of her sisters were the other three cousins. I had seen their relationship with one another on Facebook and now I could feel it. They have a strong bond connecting them; it's one of the things that has elicited such a strong sense of admiration from me.

Antoinette explained their familial connections that could not be determined by simply looking at a family tree. Her two "sisters" were actually a blood-sister and a cousin-sister. Renee was Antoinette's natural sister; their mother being Phyllis. Phyllis was Ernestina's and my father Tony's sister. Marla is Ernestina's daughter; Ernestina adopted Antoinette making Marla and Antoinette sisters. I totally love this!! This isn't the only story of the Manzanares family taking one another's children as their own. Mi casa su casa.

Zoom is not an ideal format for a first meeting as the lag time is confusing, but we muddled through and had thirty minutes of testing the waters. I hadn't known what to expect and was hoping no one would be confrontational or disparaging of Mama. I needn't have been concerned. They were so wonderful and accepting. I couldn't have imagined a warmer or more caring environment for a first meeting. We briefly discussed relationships and how they fit into our family tree. I learned my father was called "Tony Joe" or sometimes "Junior" to distinguish him from his father by the same name. The family called Ernestina "Tina" so I felt justified in calling her Tia Tina in my heart and mind.

Perhaps the most rewarding thing for me was when Marla mentioned she thought I resembled our grandmother, Tony Joe, and Tia Tina's mother, Dolorita Maria. That went straight to my core as I remembered how Dolorita's eyes penetrated mine when I first saw her photo.

The Zoom ended too quickly for me because I just couldn't get enough of my new family. I especially wanted to meet Tia Tina. She had become a sort of icon for me. I would never meet my father, Tony Joe, on this earth, but she was his sister. The closest living person to him. She had known him as a boy, had loved him as a brother, and knew him in a way I envied. I yearned for knowledge of him, I craved stories and anecdotes and pictures.

18 July 2020   Another Zoom meeting, this time Tia Tina was able to join. Finally, I could see the person not just her Facebook image; I couldn't get enough of looking at her. My father's sister. She looked beautiful and sweet. I loved her instantly. She had questions about Mama that stemmed not only from curiosity but from a place of incredulity. I recognized it for I was in that same place. She wondered about this unknown woman who had been in her brother's life. This stranger who was now claiming a place in the family. She wondered about this person who had been a part of Tony Joe's affection. We had upset each other's proverbial apple carts and we both had questions.

Tia Tina said there were many things she did not know about her brother, Tony Joe. True to the times, the family lived in several different houses on the same farm. When Tony Joe was still a small boy, Tia Tina's father, Tony Sr, picked him up and declared that he was taking his grandson to live with him, and he did. Mi casa su casa. Even though my father grew up in a different household, the family members went back and forth across the farm in a constant flow of love and affection.

Tia Tina told a few stories, and I could tell she had a great store of them. She said Tony Joe had died of heart issues which were prevalent in the Manzanares line. She also said he absolutely, unapologetically loved cows. My father was a cowboy. I loved it! I later acquired a photo of him in a white suit wearing a white hat. Of course, it was white. He was one of the good guys.

I was just beginning to accept that Tony Joe was indeed a good guy. I had undergone such heartache with Frank, such anguish and sorrow and trauma over his conduct, I could hardly believe that I did indeed have a good guy for a father.

Tia Tina joined the rest of the family in her concern about Tony Joe's wife. They had been friends and sisters-in-law for a lifetime; they had shared my father's love. How would my existence impact her? I didn't know her and still haven't met her, but I was concerned as well; I want to spare her any pain or anguish.

I had mentioned earlier to Randy's mother, Antoinette, that Mama had worked at Whitman and wondered if Tony Joe had any connections there. What she said exploded in my head and scattered spiritual celebratory confetti in my soul. Yes! Yes, Tony Joe had worked there. Tia Tina said she had even, on occasion, gone with the family to pick him up after work.

At last, I had the information that linked my parents in their unlikely association. No one remembered exactly what he did there, but he was definitely there. 1946 Colorado did not hire Mexicans, so Antonio Jose Manzanares became Italian Tony Manzan when he applied for employment. I feel in my bones that he not only fabricated his name but fudged on his age as well.

Upon learning of my new father's existence, one of the first things I did was correlate dates to my birth date. Tony Joe was fifteen when I was conceived; sixteen when I was born. WOW! Really? It shocked me in the beginning, but I later realized what a different world it was then. Boys to men was not a boy band. Boys worked hard on the farm and in the factory. Boys supported families and even went to war. Boys *were* men.

Mama was four years older but still a naïve girl trying to make her way alone in the world. Because I'm a romantic, I can see them falling in love in spite of their differences. Throwing caution to the wind to snatch a few exquisite moments together. A real-life West Side Story distorted into a sad and sorrowful ending.

CHAPTER 33

"Names are the sweetest and most important sounds in any language." Dale Carnegie

30 July 2020 For weeks now the Baader-Meinhof Phenomenon had been alive and well in my life. You know, when you get a brand-new silver Mustang then you see them everywhere? It seemed as if the name Ewing was everywhere I looked. Bank accounts, Mortgage papers, marriage certificate, social security card, employment records, Facebook, church documents, and incoming mail. Elizabeth Ewing was everywhere. Early one morning it hit me between the eyes. I wasn't a Ewing! Ewing wasn't my name. So, what was I going to do about it?

On July 30, seven weeks and two days after learning Tony Joe was my father, I marched resolutely into the county courthouse and filed to change my name to Manzanares. When I filled out the paperwork, consistent to my lifelong feelings about Ida, I left it out and became Elizabeth (first name) Manzanares (middle name) Wenig (last name). When I wrote my new name for the first time a strange feeling enveloped me. I felt a part of something wonderful. I thought of my father, Tony Joe, the good guy. I thought of my mother and how she must have loved him. I thought of Tia Tina, my dear sweet aunt. I thought of the Manzanares family and how they had drawn me in and loved me.

6 Aug 2020 I was up before the sun. Today was the day I'd get my name. My real name. The name of my father. Today I would petition the court. I would stand before a family-court judge and declare to the world my name was Manzanares.

There was only one petitioner ahead of me and before I could get nervous, I was standing before the judge. He seemed friendly and asked me a few simple questions: why did I want to change my name, why did I think Antonio was my father and were there any objections from my children? I always thought that the last question was a little strange, but it didn't matter. My children had climbed aboard this bullet train with a hunger to see my heart healed.

The Judge signed his name, rapped his gavel, looked up at me, and smiled,

> *"Elizabeth Manzanares Wenig,*
> *have a good day."*

Boy, was I having a good day.

CHAPTER 34

*"I feel the nights stretching away thousands long
behind the days till they reach the darkness where all
of me is ancestor."*
Annie Finch, <u>Spells: New and Selected Poems</u>

December 2020 The genealogy site FamilySearch has a kind of sister site called Relative Finder. I was anxious to explore it since my ancestry tree had a whole new branch. I was still feeling the sting of losing Martin Luther as a twelfth great-grandfather.

As I read through the list of progenitors a smile slowly made its way across my face. King Ferdinand and Queen Isabella of Spain, the very ones who sent Columbus on his fateful journey to discover the New World were my fourteenth great-grandparents. I couldn't wait to tell Henry.

I went on to discover many wonderful people and history in my new family. Conquistadors and explorers, Native Americans and Spaniards and Mexicans, intrepid men and women of faith and courage who did their part in founding our country.

I'm particularly enamored with Captain Roque Madrid Sebastiana Ruiz Caceras, my ninth great-grandfather. In 1692 New Mexico's governor put together an assembly of Spanish soldiers which included Captain Madrid and Pueblo Native American allies. Captain

Madrid took charge of two Pueblo Native American cousins of northern New Mexico for the purpose of reconciling them with family members. His task included returning those who were in exile and establishing peace. In the midst of this formidable assignment were the underlying efforts of restoring New Mexico to the Spanish crown. [xxxv]

Captain Madrid spent several years alongside the Pueblo and Spanish leaders trying to inaugurate a lasting peace. In 1705 he commanded an expedition against the Navajos. The campaign consisted of Spanish soldiers, citizens, and Pueblo allies eager to retaliate against the murderous Navajo raids and the kidnapping of Pueblo children.

Captain Madrid kept a meticulous journal of this excursion into Navajo territory. It is the earliest and only eyewitness account of the eighteenth-century Navajo homeland entitled <u>The Navajos in 1705 Roque Madrid's Campaign Journal.</u> [xxxvi]

As I read his journal, my heart went out to him. I was with him when New Mexico desert dust caked his clothing and parched his lips. The very fact that he was exhausted and burdened with leadership yet took the time and effort to record his privations and victories touched my own journal-writing soul. I felt the urge to write flowing in my veins brought to me through Manzanares's blood.

Captain Madrid's aptitude, a combination of leadership and compassion, prompted New Mexico's Governor Don Diego De Vargas to bestow a land grant to Ninth Great Grandfather Captain Roque Madrid in 1693.[xxxvii] Grandpa Madrid's family line not only went back to Spain but to the proud Pueblo Native American. This brings me to the beans. Yes, the beans.

The Pueblo are descendants of the Mogollon, Hohokam, and Anasazi Native Americans and is one of the oldest cultures in the United States. [xxxviii] The Anasazi cultivated a remarkable bean with high drought tolerance, a very high nutritional profile and health benefits regarding cancer, diabetes, the heart, immune system and combating inflammation. [xxxix]

Clay pots full of the "Anasazi Beans" were discovered in their celebrated cliff dwellings. Legend has it that after the beans were carted off to the museum, an uninformed worker found the beans and surreptitiously planted some of them. He remained in hot water until the beans sprouted and not only grew but reproduced. In 1993 the Anasazi Bean was trademarked and launched commercially, elevating the museum worker's blunder to breakthrough. [xl]

The term Anasazi was established in 1927 in the archaeological Pecos Classification system. The modern-day Pueblo Nation is taking issue with the Navajo term as its literal meaning is "ancient enemy" and they consider it disrespectful to refer to their ancestors in such a manner. They have changed their vernacular from Anasazi to "Ancestral Puebloan". [xli]

I understand that, but think I'll stick with Anasazi for my beans.

A friend of mine shared some Anasazi beans with me several years ago. Each season as I plant and save seeds, I think of my ancestral grandmother toiling in the hot Mesa Verde sun also planting and saving. It's one more link to my father, Tony Joe.

CHAPTER 35

> *"The presence and involvement of a father is unlike anything else in the universe. That's because dads mimic what our heavenly Father does for us, His children—He protects, shelters, comforts and loves."*
> Joe Battaglia

April 2021   Throughout the rest of the year and into the next I got to know my new kin. Tia Tina turned 90 years old in April so my husband, Gary and I traveled to Colorado to be a part of the celebration. I'd spent the last few weeks trying to memorize faces and names and relationships and trying to calm the nervous jitters in my stomach. I had Zoomed twice more and met more cousins, but this at last would be in person.

As we landed at the Denver airport, I began to think about Mama coming here to give birth to me instead of staying in Pueblo. Mama was pregnant with a Mexican baby so reason dictates I would be a brown baby. Even though a few years later my hair turned dark, at the time I was born I popped out all white and blond, and Mama went back home to Pueblo with me.

Of course, I won't know for sure until I see her in the hereafter, but this seems logical to me. I will not brood on what she would have done if I'd been born brown.

I finally decided to relax and enjoy the experience of meeting my new family. After arriving at Tia Tina's place of residence, we walked through the door and there they stood. The first three family: Antoinette—called Toni—who was Randy's mother, her husband, and the cutest, tiniest person who could only have been Tia Tina.

My first impression was that Toni and Tia Tina were so short. I'm short, and they were even shorter. It was actually more of a shock. The Ewings had all been tall, tall, tall. It never occurred to me that my height and the height of my children and grandchildren would have come partly from my Manzanares heritage. My spirit soared as they proved to be every bit of wonderful as I had imagined.

We got to have Tia Tina all to ourselves the entire day. She demonstrated her delightful, knowledgeable, and effervescent story-telling abilities throughout our tour of family history and burial places. We traveled the entire Southern end of Colorado, witnessed breathtaking mountainous scenery, and grew to love this energetic, lovely vivacious lady whom I could now call my own.

My fingers flew over my notepaper as I tried in vain to keep up with Tia Tina's stories. I wanted to remember every word, which, of course, I didn't. I finally settled for just absorbing her sweet spirit. When we reached Tony Joe's town, the town where he had lived and raised his family and was eventually buried, with Tia Tina's stories, I imagined him there. I saw him tending his cows, painting his house, and playing with his three boys. I saw him walk down the street every day to his church. I saw him sit in his pew, bow his head, and say his prayers. I wondered what it would have been like to sit beside him there, the tower bell ringing, the two of us alone with God. The two of us in church together.

We drove further up the mountain on a small dirt road that ended at the cemetery. Suddenly, after a lifetime of searching for my father, there he was. His stone silently and reverently pronounced Tony Joseph Manzanares Jr., Husband, Father, Grandfather. I thought about those roles in his life, a life in which I never played a part. But now, he plays a role in my life and the lives of my family. He is a father and a grandfather, great grandfather, and even a great-great-grandfather.

I felt a love emanating from him, radiating from worlds beyond. I felt a bond, a connection that had always flowed through my body's DNA and now flowed through my heart and my mind. I shut my eyes and held him close, feeling him near. I wished I had known him, and someday I will.

His loved ones had called him Tony Joe, or Uncle Tony…what would I call him? I couldn't call him daddy, that was reserved for Daddy Mac. Father felt too formal. Papa came to mind…Papa Joe. It felt right.

Beside Papa Joe's grave lay another: James M. Manzanares, my brother. He had been born four days after Christmas, what a joyous time that must have been. I imagined Papa Joe and his family celebrating. James' birth had been the exact month and year my baby sister, Wanda, had come into the world and left it just as abruptly. I pondered on having a sister and a brother born just over two weeks apart. My twelve-year-old self would have been over the moon happy about having two siblings; it would have fulfilled my first secret wish twice over.

James met an untimely death just three years before I stood over his grave. I felt a great loss for never having known him, grief for what might have been. Tia Tina said everyone called him Tweety. It seemed an unlikely name for a strapping Hispanic man; I know there's a good anecdote there.

> *"In every conceivable manner, the family is a link to our past, bridge to our future."* Alex Haley

We stepped out of the car, my husband Gary and I, and walked toward the festivities. My stomach tightened as I saw them, my family. Tia Tina's birthday party was just getting underway. Antoinette and her husband were at the ready with greetings and I was so grateful to at least have already met them; it softened my anxiety. I saw curious glances from others as I made my way to the guest of honor. Tia Tina was seated at a table and had already spied me. My heart gladdened when she gave me a big smile as I gave her a reciprocal hug. Antoinette gave me an introductory tour as I was trying to match Zoom and Facebook faces with real-time ones. New names and faces emerged as my family tree grew and grew...and grew.

I wondered what they were thinking. I felt like laughing and crying. I was so happy to be there, to see them and listen to them and bask in all this *family*. I felt like I was in a make-believe world. I loved meeting them, knowing I couldn't possibly remember all their names.

I met my brother, James' lovely widow, Robin, and held her in an embrace that felt like James was there, too. She loved her father-in-law and has since shared so many Papa Joe stories with me. Like Papa Joe loved Pepsi and Snickers Bars. I loved that because my daughter, Cyndi is also a fan of the Pepsi/Snicker duo. Papa Joe showed his quirky fun side by putting ice cream in cereal. And, when he had an upset stomach, he drank peppermint water. Being an herbalist and peppermint enthusiast myself, I particularly related to that herbal remedy.

Robin also shared stories of my brother, James (I love saying that...my brother...) He lost his left eye which kept him from one of his dreams...to own a Harley. He shared a trait with our father, Papa Joe, which automatically draws him into my heart...he loved children. And James loved the Godfather movies. In my fantasy world, I can see the two of us, brother and sister, binging the Godfather with him telling me all about his childhood.

Robin is a remarkable person and I look forward to knowing her better and hearing more of her memories of both my father and my brother.

My cousin Bernadette was manning the kitchen. I could tell cooking was something she loved and was good at. She later shared that when she was a girl she loved going to her Uncle Tony's house—my Papa Joe's. He called her "boonoo" and was always dressed in his signature cowboy hat, jeans, and boots. Now I had another cowboy hero to add to my childhood leading men like Hopalong Cassidy, Gene Autry, Cisco Kid and Roy Rogers.

Papa Joe's infectious smile never failed to make Bernadette feel welcome. He loved letting her and the other children help "shave the sheep" or play in the old shed in the yard. They often went on picnics, where he regaled adults and children alike with humor and comical narratives that never failed to entertain. He was the sort of man whose kindness beamed like sunshine drawing people to him with his love and warmth.

Several of my new family shared with me Papa Joe's love of children. He had a sort of secret code between him and the youngsters. He would stand silently and look around at the kids and without saying a word he would slowly move his hand up and gently tap his shirt pocket. It was a secret signal that every child recognized. Tic Tacs were forthcoming.

If you knew Papa Joe, you knew his father. Antonio Jose Manzanares, Sr. My grandfather. They shared more than the same name, they had matching characteristics and equal love of progeny. I love that my DNA is a match to this beautiful and loving lineage that is devoted to family, children, and cowboy boots.

"Family is not an important thing. It's everything." Michael J. Fox

Cousin Myra sat at a table with her family. I went over and took an empty chair beside them. They put me at ease, and I thanked Myra for all the family pictures she had shared with me a few days after I knew Papa Joe was my birth father.

I still felt bad for even thinking of the scenario that my grandmother, her great-grandmother, Dolorita Maria, had had a relationship with Mama's father, Robert. Myra was so gracious and nice and welcoming; she immediately put me at ease.

She introduced me to her family including her mom and dad. We tentatively stuck our toes in the water of my great faux pas. Everyone was comfortable with the end result, so we felt at ease in discussing what I have come to refer to as "the great grandmother gaffe."

Myra began telling the story from her side of the electronic correspondence, drawing in her mom and dad as she humorously elaborated. Her dad is Tia Tina's nephew making him one of my many first cousins that were present at the party.

When she received my text with the horrific unthinkable suggestion that Dolorita had strayed, she immediately went to her parents. Their shocked and appalled response was naturally a resounding "NO!"

They suggested very strongly cutting ties with this crazy woman who could propose such an outlandish idea just to try to prove she was part of the family. They didn't know me, or at this point want to know me. Who in their right mind would ever slander Grandmother Dolorita!

As we sat around that table and laughed about my blunder another barrier came down in my heart. Another witness was born that welcomed me into this extraordinary family.

I watched as gift after gift was presented to Tia Tina. Each family member offered their affection and devotion to this remarkable woman on her 90th birthday. She accepted each one with genuine thankfulness and love borne of a lifetime of acquaintance and intimate association. When it came time for my gift, she revealed her true nature: total acceptance, tenderness, and Christ-like inclusion. She made me feel like a Manzanares.

Every family occasion calls for pictures. It's a rule. When it came time for first cousins, I was called up and took my place in the group. Tia Tina was front and center. Posing with them sent a feeling of warmth throughout my very being. A picture sprung up in my mind. Their plaid shirt-family reunion Christmas picture that I had found on Facebook. When I first saw that photo, I had wanted so badly to know them and to be included with them. And here I was. Right in the middle of love.

As we were saying good-byes, Cousin Marla, Tia Tina's daughter, invited us to brunch at her home the next day...Easter. I loved the idea of meeting my new family on Easter weekend. It had been one year ago on Easter that I first jotted down their names.

Then she asked if we would like to attend Easter services at their church. My heart lept. Church!!! My new family went to church!! And I was going with them. I thought of my three childhood secret wishes.

One: to have siblings. CHECK.
Two: to go to church. CHECK
Three: to have a father. CHECK.

With joy resounding in my soul I could tuck that wish list away in my heart of hearts. It had been accomplished.

CHAPTER 36

"When all the dust is settled when all the crowds are gone, the things that matter are faith, family, and friends." Barbara Bush

When we were in the midst of the jovial gathering of Tia Tina's vast family, Antoinette drew me aside. She looked intently into my eyes and said,

"I just want you to know that I believe if Uncle Tony had known about you, he would have come for you."

Her words penetrated a place already swarming with tender emotions, pulsing with poignant feelings. But this, this was so personal, as if it came directly from my father. There were so many times as a little girl I thought about him—that man out there somewhere who gave me life. Fantasized that he would be kind and loving and happy. Wished and hoped that he could love me, and we could be a family.

Antoinette had given me a very special gift.

My "heart was moved as the trees of the wood are moved with the wind." Isaiah 7:2

Her sentiment is still nestled deep in my spirit, a nucleus of essence radiating a love I've waited for all my life. I don't know if it's true, but for right now it links me to Papa Joe in a way that is healing and restorative.

I marvel at the events that have brought me to this place. I think of the many, many daddy trails I have explored. The excruciatingly painful black holes of heartache finally leading to the celestial realms of joy and peace. I could not have done it without the silent invisible omniscient help of my Savior. I am eternally thankful to the depths of my soul and beyond words to have at long last found my father.

Standing in the cemetery at their graves, Papa Joe, my father and James, my brother, I look up. There on the horizon rises the majestic twin peaks that have stood guard over this range of mountains for eons of time. Native Americans came here to gather local medicinal herbs.[xlii] My very essence that loves all plant life, especially herbs resonated with this ancient practice. I longed to explore those mounts and valleys to search for special gifts of healing planted there by our Maker.

The two mountains have many names (kind of like me) among them Dos Hermanos (Two Brothers), Twin Peaks, or Mexican Mountains.[xliii] But I am partial to the one Tia Tina shared with me that day we went exploring. The one they were first called by the Native Americans who came searching for healing herbs. The one the locals reverently softly say when they stand on their land with the cool Colorado breeze blowing across their face, the sun just peeking at a new day: Wahatoya…breasts of the earth.[xliv]

I looked down at my father and my brother, said good-by for now, and left them

Durmiendo bajo las Wahatoya.
Sleeping under the Breasts of the Earth.

THE END

EPILOGUE

Writing "Daddy Trails" has been cathartic; it has freed me in ways unimaginable. Actually getting published is stomach-clenching scary. Strangers will know what's in my closet, family and friends may see me differently, treat me differently because I've shared some intimate unsavory details of my life.

But in my heart of hearts, I believe that not only does my story reveal that shining hope and gleaming faith can be present in the face of adversity it shows that forgiveness is possible even when we think it's impossible. *Especially* when we think it's impossible.

My lifelong wishes were actually prayers. I believe the granting of my wish #3—my prayer of finding my real father—came to pass *because* I was <u>willing</u> to forgive my first two fathers and was actually <u>able</u> to forgive them with the help and through the grace of my Lord Jesus Christ.

ABOUT THE AUTHOR

Elizabeth lives in the country with her husband, Gary, her loyal dog, Toby, a gaggle of cats, a couple of chickens, her thirteen year old sour dough starter named MaryJane, her twenty-two year old bonsai Ficus she calls Annie, and her Faith garden and many plants. Her three children, nine grandchildren, and two great-grandchildren are the apple of her eye and she takes pleasure in reading, writing, and worshiping her Savior.

You can reach Elizabeth through her author page

www.lizzysfeatherpen.com

ENDNOTES

[i] Paddlefish Field Guide: Status

https://mdc.mo.gov/discover-nature/field-guide/paddlefish

[ii] https://en.wikipedia.org/wiki/Paddlefish

[iii] The Rising Sun dawns on Guam by Tony Palomo
https://www.nps.gov/parkhistory/online_books/npswapa/extContent/Lib/liberation4.htm>

[iv] Song of hope, song of faith *By Joseph Santo Tomas*
https://www.nps.gov/parkhistory/online_books/npswapa/extContent/Lib/liberation8.htm>

[v] Liberating Guam By Dave Lotz and Rose S.N. Manibusan
https://www.nps.gov/parkhistory/online_books/npswapa/extContent/Lib/liberation4.htm>

[vi] The Rising Sun dawns on Guam by Tony Palomo
https://www.nps.gov/parkhistory/online_books/npswapa/extContent/Lib/liberation4.htm

[vii] Liberating Guam   By Dave Lotz and Rose S.N. Manibusan
https://www.nps.gov/parkhistory/online_books/npswapa/extContent/L

ib/liberation16.htm

[viii] **Wikipedia** *https://en.wikipedia.org/wiki/Battle_of_Guam_(1944)>*

[ix] The Island War, by Frank O. Hough; Liberating Guam By Dave Lotz and Rose S.N. Manibusan
https://www.nps.gov/parkhistory/online_books/npswapa/extContent/Lib/liberation16.htm>

[x] Goodreads *https://www.goodreads.com/quotes/143214-the-soldier-is-the-army-no-army-is-better-than*

[xi] Liberating Guam By Dave Lotz and Rose S.N. Manibusan
https://www.nps.gov/parkhistory/online_books/npswapa/extContent/Lib/liberation16.htm>

[xii] Liberating Guam By Dave Lotz and Rose S.N. Manibusan
https://www.nps.gov/parkhistory/online_books/npswapa/extContent/Lib/liberation16.htm>

[xiii] War in The Pacific *https://www.nps.gov/wapa/planyourvisit/asan-beach-unit.htm*

[xiv] Rising Sun dawns on Guam *By Tony Palmo*
<https://www.nps.gov/parkhistory/online_books/npswapa/extContent/Lib/liberation4.htm

[xv] The Journey to Manengon by Ricardo J. Bordallo and C. Sablan Gault
<https://www.nps.gov/parkhistory/online_books/npswapa/extContent/Lib/liberation12.htm

[xvi] Liberating Guam *By Dave Lotz and Rose S.N. Manibusan*
https://www.nps.gov/parkhistory/online_books/npswapa/extContent/Lib/liberation16.htm

[xvii] **Battle of Guam**
https://en.wikipedia.org/wiki/Battle_of_Guam_(1944)>

[xviii] **Hitting the Beaches**
https://warfarehistorynetwork.com/2018/12/25/liberating-guam/>

[xix] **History of Guam** https://en.wikipedia.org/wiki/History_of_Guam

[xx] **Asan Beach Unit** <https://www.nps.gov/wapa/planyourvisit/asan-beach-unit.htm>

[xxi]**Liberating Guam By Dave Lotz and Rose S.N. Manibusan**
https://www.nps.gov/parkhistory/online_books/npswapa/extContent/Lib/liberation16.htm>

[xxii] **Military History**
https://military-history.fandom.com/wiki/Type_96_25_mm_AT/AA_Gun>

[xxiii] **Asan Beach Unit** https://www.nps.gov/wapa/planyourvisit/asan-beach-unit.htm>

[xxiv] **USS Solace - wiki** https://en.wikipedia.org/wiki/USS_Solace_(AH-5)>

[xxv] **Life Expectancy of a Tail** Gunner https://almazrestaurant.com/what-was-the-life-expectancy-of-a-tail-gunner/>

[xxvi]**Americas Aerial Gunners by Khalid Elhassan**
https://almazrestaurant.com/what-was-the-life-expectancy-of-a-tail-gunner/>

[xxvii] **The Rear Gunner 1943**
https://www.themoviedb.org/movie/100824-the-rear-gunner>

[xxviii] Joseph McCarthy Wiki
https://en.wikipedia.org/wiki/Joseph_McCarthy>

[xxix] Online Auction: Whitman 1940 Hotel postcard
https://www.listia.com/auction/60241503-used-1940-hotel-whitman-pueblo-co>

Pinterest Whitman Matchbook Cover https://www.pinterest.ca › pin › 763993524292066504

[xxx] Detective Magazine September 1965

[xxxi] Southern Illinoisan Newspaper April 1, 1965

[xxxii] Southern Illinoisan Newspaper April 2, 1965

[xxxiii] Southern Illinoisan Newspaper April 1965

[xxxiv] The Globe Democrat Sunday Magazine July 23, 1967 "The Life of a Lifer" by Shirley Althoff

[xxxv] Tupatu and Vargas Accords 1692-Orchestrating Peace in a Time of Uncertainty 1692-1696 by Jose Antonio Esquibel   EL Palacio, Spring 2006, Vol. 111, No. 1:16-18   www.elpalacio.org

[xxxvi] "The Navajos in 1705 Roque Madrid's Campaign Journal" edited, annotated and translated by Rick Hendricks and John P. Wilson

[xxxvii][xxxvii] History – Land Grant The Agua Fria Village Association (AFVA) on behalf of the Agua Fria Village Traditional Historic Community (THC) developed the Agua Fria Community Plan adopted in Resolution 2006-116 by the Santa Fe Board of County Commissioners March 13, 2007.

[xxxviii] Pueblo Native Americans: Their History, Culture and Tradition

https://blog.nativehope.org/pueblo-native-americans-their-history-culture-and-traditions>

[xxxix] Superfood For Health-Anasazi Beans
https://powerfoodhealth.com/superfoods-for-health/anasazi-beans-the-native-american-bean-that-fights-cancer-and-diabetes/>

[xl] The Anasazi Bean: A Native American Secret
https://blog.131method.com/anasazi-beans-a-native-american-secret/>

[xli] Indian Pueblo Cultural Center "What Does Anasazi Mean."
https://indianpueblo.org/what-does-anasazi-mean-and-why-is-it-controversial/

[xlii] Spanish Peaks Country Uptop Historic District
https://spanishpeakscountry.com/uptop-historic-district/

[xliii] Spanish Peaks Country A Peoples History of the Spanish Peaks
https://spanishpeakscountry.com/a-peoples-history-of-the-spanish-peaks/

[xliv] Spanish Peaks Country A Peoples History of the Spanish Peaks
https://spanishpeakscountry.com/a-peoples-history-of-the-spanish-peaks/

Made in the USA
Middletown, DE
04 December 2023